# Don Weekes

# Rockin' HOCKEY TRIVIA

GREYSTONE BOOKS
Douglas & McIntyre Publishing Group
Vancouver/Toronto/New York

*For Uncle Russell, who took me to see Maurice Richard and Jean Béliveau play at the Montreal Forum.*—Don Weekes

Copyright © 2000 by Don Weekes
00 01 02 03 04   5 4 3 2 1

Greystone Books
A division of Douglas & McIntyre Ltd.
2323 Quebec Street, Suite 201
Vancouver, British Columbia
V5T 4S7

CANADIAN CATALOGUING IN PUBLICATION DATA
    Weekes, Don.
    Rockin' hockey trivia

    ISBN 1-55054-799-2
    1. National Hockey League—Miscellanea. 2. Hockey—Miscellanea. I. Title.
GV847.W367 2000      796.962'64      C00-910553-0

Editing by Anne Rose and Kerry Banks
Typeset by Tanya Lloyd/Spotlight Designs
Cover design by Peter Cocking
Cover photograph by Scott Levy/Bruce Bennett Studios
Printed and bound in Canada by Transcontinental Printers

We gratefully acknowledge the financial support of the Canada Council for the Arts, the British Columbia Ministry of Tourism, Small Business and Culture, and the Government of Canada through the Book Publishing Industry Development Program (BPDIP) for its publishing activities.

**Don Weekes** *is a television producer and writer with* CFCF 12 *in Montreal. This is his sixteenth hockey trivia book.*

# CONTENTS

# PREFACE

If the NHL ever decides to award the Bill Masterton Trophy to a non-NHL player for his perseverance, sportsmanship and dedication to hockey, a strong candidate for consideration would be Floyd Whitney, the longtime practice goalie of the Edmonton Oilers. Whitney, father of Florida Panthers forward Ray Whitney, has toiled 17 seasons between the practice pipes, stopping rubber fired by the likes of Wayne Gretzky, Mark Messier and Doug Weight.

The sting of body welts, bruises and ice packs have almost been worth it considering the talent behind the shots, but the 46-year-old Edmonton police sergeant still dreams of backstopping the Oilers in an actual NHL game. Whitney almost got his big break December 21, 1999, when Bill Ranford went down with a foot injury in the first period of an Edmonton-Washington game. Oilers goalie Tommy Salo filled in and Whitney was paged over the Skyreach PA system, then reached by cell phone at the station.

Whitney signed a contract, suited up and then paced for two periods in the dressing room, waiting the agonizing wait. "Heck, I would have been tickled just to sit on the bench," said Whitney. "MacTee [assistant coach Craig MacTavish] and Slats [general manager Glen Sather] were pushing for me, but Kevin [coach Kevin Lowe] was worried that it might send the wrong message to the Caps."

Lowe, the consummate pro, kept his practice goalie from view out of respect for the Washington Capitals, who were being trounced at the time by the Oilers. "Kevin didn't want to rub it in," Whitney said, without a hint of regret.

As it happened, with three minutes remaining in the game Salo almost yanked himself because of a pulled groin, but kept playing, not realizing that Whitney was ready to go in. "When my son, Ray, heard about my near-game, he said, 'Boy, you would have seen some team defense then!'"

Although Whitney earns his goalie lumps for free, there have been "a few perks over the years," including some road trips and two Stanley Cup rings.

There are dozens of wonderful stories that make hockey a game for everyone—a game where anything can happen, not just to the big guys but to all of us. In our 16th hockey trivia book, we look at those big guys and the Floyd Whitneys of the hockey world. They, too, deserve their own trophies.

DON WEEKES
May 2000

# 1
# PUMPED

During the pregame warmup in the 1967 semifinals between Toronto and Chicago, Bobby Hull slapped a wicked shot over the end boards and into the private booth of Maple Leafs owner Harold Ballard. The misdirected blast struck Ballard's nose and broke it in three places. Hull was definitely pumped for the series, but his Hawks still lost in six. In this warmup we fire off a slew of questions to get you primed for the upcoming trivia chapters. Remember, stay focussed, and keep your head up!

(*Answers are on page 7*)

**1.1**  **On average, how many pucks are used in an NHL game?**
A.  Less than five pucks
B.  Between five and 10 pucks
C.  Between 10 and 20 pucks
D.  More than 20 pucks

**1.2**  **Five months after his retirement in 1999, Wayne Gretzky said he would have put off retiring for a chance to play with which player?**
A.  Jaromir Jagr
B.  Mark Messier
C.  Pavel Bure
D.  Steve Yzerman

**1.3** At the time of his January 1999 trade from the Vancouver Canucks to the Florida Panthers, Pavel Bure had scored a goal against every other NHL team except one. Which team blanked Bure?
   A. The Florida Panthers
   B. The Philadelphia Flyers
   C. The Ottawa Senators
   D. The Detroit Red Wings

**1.4** American-born Bobby Carpenter claims a number of NHL firsts in his career. Which "first" below is not his to claim?
   A. He was the first American drafted in the first round
   B. He was the first high schooler to go directly into the NHL
   C. He was the first U.S.-born player to lead the NHL in goal scoring
   D. He was the first American to score 50 goals in a season

**1.5** When Ray Bourque was traded in March 2000, which player then became the longest-serving still-active NHLer in games played with one team?
   A. New Jersey's Ken Daneyko
   B. Detroit's Steve Yzerman
   C. Minnesota's Mike Modano
   D. New York's Brian Leetch

**1.6** What was the most number of shots taken by an NHLer who went goal-less in 1999–2000?
   A. Less than 60 shots
   B. Between 60 and 70 shots
   C. Between 70 and 80 shots
   D. More than 80 shots

**1.7** Which NHL coach won 200 games in the fewest number of games?

A. Don Cherry

B. Toe Blake

C. Mike Keenan

D. Ken Hitchcock

**1.8** Players often have incentive clauses in their contracts for goals or points scored in a season. How much bonus money was riding on St. Louis' Scott Young and his final shot on goal during the 1998–99 season?

A. $200,000

B. $400,000

C. $600,000

D. $800,000

**1.9** Who was "Lefty" Wilson?

A. A pro baseball pitcher turned NHL star in the 1940s

B. A famous Boston team doctor

C. A New York mobster who ran Madison Square Garden

D. A longtime practice goalie for Detroit

**1.10** Which NHL 500-goal scorer is known as "The Little Ball of Hate"?

A. Dino Ciccarelli

B. Pat Verbeek

C. Brett Hull

D. Theo Fleury

**1.11** Which NHLer delivered the most hits in 1998–99, the year the league first recorded hits as a statistic?

A. Gary Roberts

B. Darren McCarty

C. Bobby Holik

D. Chris Pronger

**1.12** What is the unofficial NHL record for the worst plus-minus by a player in one season?
   A. Less than minus 40
   B. Between minus 40 and minus 60
   C. Between minus 60 and minus 80
   D. More than minus 80

**1.13** If Mario Lemieux holds the NHL mark for most shorthanded goals in a season (13 goals), what is the record for most short-handed goals by an individual in *one game*?
   A. No player has ever scored more than one shorthanded goal in a game
   B. Two shorthanded goals
   C. Three shorthanded goals
   D. Four shorthanded goals

**1.14** What is the most number of points scored by a player who played only one NHL season?
   A. 48 points
   B. 58 points
   C. 68 points
   D. 78 points

**1.15** What is the most points scored by an Original Six (pre-1967 expansion) player in his final NHL season?
   A. 43 points
   B. 53 points
   C. 63 points
   D. 73 points

1.16 What is the highest point total by a runner-up in the NHL scoring race?
A. 78 points
B. 108 points
C. 138 points
D. 168 points

1.17 What is the NHL record for most points in a season by a player who collected zero minutes in penalties?
A. 34 points
B. 44 points
C. 54 points
D. 64 points

1.18 What is the most senior age at which an NHLer has recorded a 100-point season?
A. Less than 33 years old
B. 33 to 36 years old
C. 37 to 40 years old
D. More than 40 years old

1.19 Which of the following NHL records is held by a rookie?
A. Most points by a player in one period
B. Most assists by a left-winger in one season
C. Most points by a defenseman in one game
D. Most goals by a right-winger in one season

1.20 Which NHLer is considered to hold the longest streak for scoring or assisting on consecutive goals scored by his team?
A. Pittsburgh's Jaromir Jagr
B. Edmonton's Wayne Gretzky
C. Pittsburgh's Mario Lemieux
D. Detroit's Steve Yzerman

**1.21** After Canada and the United States, what is the third most represented country in the NHL?

A. The Czech Republic
B. Sweden
C. Russia
D. Finland

**1.22** Which superstar sniper scored the last NHL goal of the millennium?

A. Eric Lindros
B. Brett Hull
C. Paul Kariya
D. Jaromir Jagr

**1.23** How many of the six Sutter brothers became team captains in the NHL?

A. Only one, Brian
B. Three
C. Four
D. All six brothers

**1.24** What is the most penalty-free seasons played by an NHL skater?

A. One season
B. Three seasons
C. Five seasons
D. Seven seasons

**1.25** Aside from Jaromir Jagr, how many of the 32 former NHL scoring champions are in the Hockey Hall of Fame?

A. All but one
B. 12
C. 22
D. All 32 scoring champs

**1.26** According to the *Philadelphia Inquirer*, how much money has Flyers general manager Bobby Clarke blown on bad player deals?
A.  U.S.$6 million
B.  U.S.$16 million
C.  U.S.$26 million
D.  U.S.$36 million

**1.27** Owen Nolan was nicknamed "Buster" after whom?
A.  Comedian Buster Keaton
B.  Buster the Clown
C.  Buster, Nolan's pet bull terrier
D.  Boxer Buster Douglas

# PUMPED
## Answers

**1.1**  **D.  More than 20 pucks**
Pucks usually have a game existence measured in seconds or minutes. According to the NHL, between 20 and 40 pucks are used through three periods of play. Has any puck ever survived an entire game? Only in one documented case during the league's modern era. On November 10, 1979, the Minnesota North Stars and the Los Angeles Kings played to a 6–6 tie at the Great Western Forum, and only one puck was used during the match. Such longevity is rare considering pucks are either lost to the crowd or replaced by the referee once they thaw. (Pucks are kept frozen for swifter movement and truer bounce during games.)

**1.2**  **C.  Pavel Bure**
Wayne Gretzky probably would have extended his playing career another year for a chance to play with a Jagr, Yzerman or Messier, but in a TSN interview in November 1999, the Great One said:

"If (the Rangers) would have traded for Pavel Bure last year, I probably would still be playing right now." Instead Bure went from Vancouver to the Florida Panthers, where he scored a league-high 58 goals in 1999–2000. Meanwhile the Rangers, minus Gretzky, spent U.S.$61 million and still finished 23rd overall. When Panthers executive Bill Torrey heard Gretzky's remarks about staying another year to play with Bure, he said, "You know, I can arrange that."

**1.3    A.   The Florida Panthers**
Players are often acquired in trades by teams that they have tormented on the ice. But this wasn't the case in the Bure-to-Florida deal. The only team the Russian Rocket had failed to score a goal against was the Panthers. In five career games against Florida, Bure managed only four assists.

**1.4    C.   He was the first U.S.-born player to lead the NHL in goal scoring**
Carpenter wasn't the first American to lead the league in goals (Keith Tkachuk did it first in 1996–97), but he can take credit for being the first American NHLer drafted in the first round (third overall in 1981); the first high schooler to go directly to the NHL (from St. John's Prep to the NHL in 1981–82); and the first American to record a 50-goal season (53 goals in 1983–84).

**1.5    B.   Detroit's Steve Yzerman**
It was unthinkable—Ray Bourque in a uniform other than the black and gold of his beloved Bs. After almost 21 seasons, 18 All-Star selections, five Norris Trophies as the NHL's best defenseman and a Calder Trophy as top rookie, Bourque was finally traded to a Stanley Cup contender—the Colorado Avalanche—at his request. Four teams, including Philadelphia (his first choice), made a pitch for the future Hall-of-Fame rearguard, but the Avalanche pulled the trigger and bagged Bourque for the playoff drive. (Interestingly, it was Patrick Roy who laid the groundwork

for the Avalanche, by selling Bourque on the idea of coming to Colorado when they were teammates playing for Canada at the 1998 Olympics.) Of course, the trade wasn't completely unexpected. During the mid-1990s, Bourque settled for less money to stay in Boston, expecting that the Bruins would turn the corner. But as things in Beantown went from bad to worse, it looked like the veteran had made the wrong decision. Bourque could have signed as an unrestricted free agent with Detroit and won two Stanley Cups by the time he was finally dealt to Colorado in 2000. His departure left Ken Daneyko and Steve Yzerman as the longest-serving active players in the league. At season's end, each played 17 seasons with their respective teams: Yzerman suited up in 1,253 games, and Daneyko, 1,070. Leetch served 13 years; Modano, 12.

## 1.6   C.  Between 70 and 80 shots

A number of NHLers recorded the worst possible shooting percentage—0.00—in league action in 1999–2000, but New Jersey's Ken Daneyko suffered the greatest level of frustration, blasting away on net 74 times without a goal. Other white-washed players included Tampa's Cory Sarich (no goals on 69 shots) and Rhett Warrener (no goals on 68 shots). Among one-goal scorers, the worst shooting percentage belonged to Jamie Rivers of the New York Islanders, who scored once on 95 shots for an awful 1.1 percentage.

## 1.7   A.  Don Cherry

When Dallas Stars coach Ken Hitchcock won his 200th game on March 12, 2000, the sports pages reported a surprising bit of trivia about Canada's favourite redneck broadcaster, Don Cherry. Although Hitchcock reached the 200-win mark in 358 games, he was only the fifth-fastest in NHL history and 16 games back of Cherry, the fastest 200-win coach ever. Old-time bench boss Toe Blake needed 345 games; Tommy Ivan, 353; and Mike Keenan and Ken Hitchcock, 357. Interestingly, Keenan was the only coach among the five to reach his 200th victory split between two teams (Philadelphia and Chicago).

**1.8   D. $800,000**
On April 18, 1999, in the Blues' last regular-season match, Pavol Demitra needed one point to hit the 90-point plateau and activate a $500,000 incentive clause in his contract. With time running out and St. Louis ahead 3–2, Demitra passed up an open net opportunity and fed the puck to Scott Young, who was one goal short of the 25 he needed to collect on his own $300,000 bonus. Unfortunately, neither man benefited from Demitra's generosity. Young's shot was blocked by Los Angeles defenseman Jaroslav Modry. Asked how he could pass up a certain half-million, Demitra said, "Scott needed a goal." Worse still, earlier in the game, Demitra almost had his 90th point when he assisted on a goal by Lubos Bartecko. The goal was called back after video replay determined Bartecko was in the crease.

**1.9   D.  A longtime practice goalie for Detroit**
Before the two-goalie system, teams found spare goalies wherever they could; in Detroit they relied on "Lefty" Wilson, a trainer and practice goaltender who actually played three NHL games. Wilson tended nets in his first game on October 10, 1953, replacing an injured Terry Sawchuk in period three of a 4–1 loss to Montreal. He played twice more in league action. Oddly, both times he faced his own team, the Red Wings. Wilson was loaned to Toronto to replace an injured Harry Lumley on January 23, 1956, and to Boston to sub for an injured Don Simmons on December 29, 1957. Lefty's career consisted of three games for three different teams—twice against his own team!

**1.10   B.  Pat Verbeek**
It might just be the way he plays, full of emotion and dirty tricks, but, somewhere along the way, Verbeek picked up the nickname "The Little Ball of Hate." Actually, the dubbing came courtesy of

goalie Glenn Healy in the mid-1990s, while the pair were with the New York Rangers. At five foot nine, 190 pounds, Verbeek is all fire and brimstone; he sparked Detroit's number one line of Steve Yzerman and Brendon Shanahan during the 1999–2000 season. His 500th came on March 22, 2000, in a two-goal performance in a 2–2 knot against Calgary. The Little Ball of Hate, a third-liner on the 1999 Dallas Cup winners, couldn't contain himself as he jumped up and down and pumped his fist into the air. Verbeek's 500th was set by Yzerman, another charter member of the 500-goal club.

1.11 **A. Gary Roberts**
The NHL finally entered the computer age in the late 1990s, a move not made soon enough for North America's statistic-mad sports fans. Hockey fans can now feast on a variety of crunched numbers, from ice time to legal hits. In this last category, Carolina's Gary Roberts led the NHL with 260 hits on opposing players in 1998–99.

## THE NHL's TOP HIT MEN IN 1998–99

| Player | Team | GP | Hits |
| --- | --- | --- | --- |
| Gary Roberts | Carolina | 77 | 260 |
| Ken Klee | Washington | 78 | 248 |
| Mattias Norstrom | Los Angeles | 78 | 236 |
| Bob Boughner | Nashville | 79 | 233 |
| Rade Bonk | Ottawa | 81 | 225 |
| Daniel McGillis | Philadelphia | 78 | 220 |

1.12 **D. More than minus 80**
Forgotten Bill Mikkelson's claim to fame is his plus-minus record, the worst in NHL history at minus 82. He earned the record in 1974–75 with the Washington Capitals, a team so bad it

finished with only eight wins and five ties while suffering through 67 losses. The 1974–75 Caps also belong in the books, with the mark for the fewest points (21) in a 70-game schedule and the lowest winning percentage (.131) ever. Through it all, or at least for 59 games that season, Mikkelson suffered along with the Capitals and feels his record is rock-solid. "It will be a hard one to beat, and why would you want to beat it?" he said in a 2000 *National Post* story. Today Mikkelson works in Edmonton as an executive for IBM.

**1.13  C.  Three shorthanded goals**
On March 9, 1991, Calgary's Theo Fleury set a league record by notching an unprecedented three shorthanded goals against St. Louis in an 8–4 win. Curiously, the two Flames who were credited with assists on Fleury's first shorthanded goal, Frank Musil and Stephane Matteau, played a large part in Fleury's second and third shorthanders. Musil was the Calgary player penalized when Fleury scored his second shorthanded goal; Matteau was in the box for Fleury's historic third. The shorthanded hat trick, an NHL first, included Fleury's 42nd, 43rd and 44th goals of the season.

**1.14  A.  48 points**
The NHL record book is dotted with hundreds of one-year washouts, most of whom never racked up more than a few games or points in their brief big-league careers. Washington's Milan Novy would be an exception among those castoffs. A three-time Czechoslovakian player of the year (1977, 1981 and 1982), Novy was drafted by the Capitals in 1982, played the 1982–83 season as a 31-year-old rookie and scored 18 goals and 48 points, a mark unequalled among one-year players. The following season he returned to his native country, never to skate in NHL action again.

**1.15  B.  53 points**

Perhaps no NHLer from the six-team era quit the game at a higher level than Syl Apps, the inspirational leader of the Toronto Maple Leafs during the 1930s and 1940s. Apps captained the Leafs through six seasons and three Stanley Cups before retiring in 1948 with the best season total of his 10-year career, 53 points. A superb two-way centre, Apps went out on top, promising to retire once he scored 200 goals. In his final regular-season game on March 21, 1948, he notched a hat trick: the 199th, 200th and 201st goals of his illustrious career. Later that spring, he led Toronto to the Stanley Cup in a sweep over Detroit. Apps scored in the Cup's final game.

**1.16  D. 168 points**

In Wayne Gretzky's first season in Los Angeles, the Great One amassed 168 points, a high number, but only good enough for second place to league leader Mario Lemieux's career year of 199 points in 1988–89. In fact, Lemieux made a career out of stealing thunder, outscoring the totals of the three runners-up in his Art Ross years. Mario, with 161 points, bested Jaromir Jagr's 149 points in 1995–96; in 1987–88 he beat Gretzky's 149-point total with a 168-point year; and he captured the headlines in 1992–93 by amassing 160 points in just 60 games to top Pat LaFontaine's career best of 148 points.

**1.17  C.  54 points**

This mark is shared by teammates. In 1944–45, Bill Mosienko and Clint Smith of the Chicago Blackhawks both notched 54 points without making a single visit to the sin bin, a record high for unpenalized players. Mosienko won the Lady Byng Trophy for most gentlemanly player that year. Smith, who accumulated only 24 penalty minutes in 483 career games, won the award on two previous occasions.

**1.18** **D. More than 40 years old**

This mark could only belong to Mr. Hockey, Gordie Howe. During his remarkable NHL career, Howe scored 1,850 points but had just one century season. It came in 1968–69, when Howe was still in his prime, at age 41. He accumulated 103 points, but his most famous marker that year was his 700th goal (a league first), which he scored on December 4 in a 7–2 win over Pittsburgh.

**1.19** **B. Most assists by a left-winger in one season**

In 1992–93, Boston Bruins rookie Joe Juneau collected 70 assists to break Kevin Stevens's single-season record of 69 assists by a left-winger. Despite his stellar freshman campaign, Juneau did not win the Calder Trophy that year. His performance was overshadowed by Winnipeg's Teemu Selanne, who became the league's most prolific rookie marksman with 76 goals and 132 points.

**1.20** **A. Pittsburgh's Jaromir Jagr**

Although the issue has not been conclusively researched, it is believed that Jagr leads all NHLers after scoring or assisting on 15 consecutive goals scored by the Pittsburgh Penguins between October 16 and November 4, 1999. Jagr's streak earned him seven goals and eight assists in seven games. Interestingly, during the same period the Penguins remained winless, losing five and tying two. The biggest beneficiary was Robert Lang, who scored five goals and two assists off Jagr's stick. During January 1989, Mario Lemieux scored or assisted on 14 consecutive Pittsburgh goals; Wayne Gretzky's personal best was 13, with the Kings in 1991–92.

**1.21** **A. The Czech Republic**

No North American sport has gone through the dramatic transition experienced by the NHL in the 1980s and 1990s; the European player, once an exception in the time of Bobby Orr and

Guy Lafleur, has changed the face of the league and, to some extent, its style of play. In the 30-team NHL more than one in every four players (28 per cent) comes from Europe. In 1999–2000, the Czech Republic, with 50, had the highest number of Euro-NHLers. Russia had 47, Sweden 37, Finland 22 and Slovakia 10.

### 1.22  B.  Brett Hull

Brett Hull scored the last goal of the millennium in his typical, dramatic fashion. In only one of two NHL games scheduled December 31, 1999, Hull got the tying and winning goals in the third period of a 5–4 Dallas victory over the Mighty Ducks—Hull's 600th and 601st career goals. He scored them in his 900th game, a personal objective for Hull since the season began. "I wanted 600 in 900 games because they're round numbers and it's easier to do the math," joked Hull. The Stars' right-winger scored number 600 from the high slot on the power play, when he took a pass from Kirk Muller and fired a sizzler past goalie Guy Hebert. Hull added the winning goal two minutes later, his 601st, the game winner and the last goal of the millennium. It came at 8:49 of the third frame, approximately 9:30 p.m. central time in Dallas. "It's a neat thing, scoring the last goal of the millennium in the NHL," said Hull.

### 1.23  C.  Four

No one can ever question the heart of the Sutter gang. Among the six siblings from Viking, Alberta, four became NHL captains: Brian spent nine seasons wearing the "C" in St. Louis (1979–80 to 1987–88); brother Brent, five seasons in Long Island (1987–88 to 1991–92); brother Ron, two years in Philadelphia (1989–90 to 1990–91); and brother Darryl, five years in Chicago (1982–83 to 1986–87).

**1.24  C.  Five seasons**

In 820 games over 13 NHL seasons, Val Fonteyne sat in the cooler for just 26 minutes. That's an average of a two-minute infraction once every year. The Detroit, New York and Pittsburgh winger recorded an amazing five penalty-clean seasons between 1959–60 and 1971–72, and he never earned more than four penalty minutes in a year. To put Fonteyne's box time in perspective, choirboy 18-year veteran Dave Keon played like a thug, totalling 116 minutes of penalties—almost four times Fonteyne's numbers.

**1.25  A.  All but one**

Not that there is an unwritten rule or a rubber stamp somewhere for NHL scoring leaders, but based on the history books, all Art Ross winners, sooner or later, make it into hockey's hallowed Hall. It's been the case for every title holder, from Joe Malone to Wayne Gretzky, with one exception: Herb Cain of the Boston Bruins. Cain was 1943–44's scoring champion and, aside from the still-active Jaromir Jagr, he is the only points leader not inducted into the Hockey Hall of Fame. Unfortunately, this may be Cain's biggest claim to fame. He was certainly no Bobby Orr or Wayne Gretzky. Although he did produce Gretzky-like totals (82 points in 48 games in his title year), the rub against Cain may be his overall record. His previous career-high was 36 points, and he never netted more than 45 after winning the scoring race. The NHL was also depleted of quality skaters and goalies during the war years, which may have tarnished Cain's crown. Nevertheless, he won two Stanley Cups, one with the Montreal Maroons in 1935 and another with Boston in 1941, as part of the Cain-Cowley-Hill line. Although the unit played second fiddle to the Bruins' Kraut Line, it had a prominent role in the championship. During his 13-year career, Herb Cain scored 400 points in 570 games.

**1.26 C. U.S.$26 million**

*Philadelphia Inquirer* reporter Tim Panaccio calculated Bobby Clarke blew U.S.$26 million on players who either didn't play with, or who made little contribution to, the Flyers. Clarke, in his greatest deal, did steal heavyweights John LeClair and Eric Desjardins from Montreal, but his record after that point is abysmal. He paid out $9 million up-front money to Chris Gratton, only to send him back later to Tampa Bay; $1.9 million to underachiever Alexandre Daigle; $2.6 million for one season (minus the playoffs) to Paul Coffee; almost a half-million to minor-leaguer Roman Vopat; and $12.6 million for five years to Luke Richardson, the team's fifth or sixth defenseman.

**1.27 D. Boxer Buster Douglas**

Owen Nolan has always had a mean streak. Try finding out about his nickname, "Buster," and you're met with an icy glare as intimidating as his bruising style of play. But according to Nolan's former agent Gene McBurney, the moniker comes from one-time world heavyweight champion Buster Douglas. McBurney says Nolan earned it in his rookie season, 1990–91, the same year Buster Douglas beat up Mike Tyson in a match in Toyko. "They gave it to [Nolan] in Quebec, because he liked to fight," McBurney told the *Edmonton Journal*. Owen, consider the subject closed.

## Game 1

# HOCKEY CROSSWORD 1

*(Solutions are on page 120)*

**Across**

1. Team from California (3 words)

9. A player's nick _____

10. Cam _____

12. _____ Gilbert

14. Ontario Hockey League (abbr.)

15. Spills and _____

16. After a shift: He's _____ to the bench

18. 1980s Montreal D-man Rick _____

20. _____ Clapper

21. Dirty player

23. Goon Chris _____

24. Rock's Elvis _____

28. Coach _____ Arbour

29. Team _____

30. Opposite to win

32. An order: Salary _____

34. Overtime (abbr.)

35. _____ Langway

36. Come from _____

37. Playing surface

39. Broadcaster Dick _____

40. _____ Lafleur

41. Catch a _____

42. _____ Belfour

**Down**

1. The Flyers' Pelle _____

2. Montreal's Turner _____

3. Opposite of late

4. A play from coast to coast (4 words)

5. Who's _____ goal tonight?

6. 1980s Montreal's Mats _____

7. General manager (abbr.)

8. He establishes or _____ the record

11. Opposite of old

13. After this point players can not be traded (2 words)

16. _____ shoots, he scores

17. 1980s North Star D-man, Curt _____

19. Old Hab Kenny _____

22. Paul Kariya's number

25. Dallas' Craig _____

26. 1990s Calgary D-man, Trent _____

27. Hakan _____

28. Morning

31. _____ Yzerman

33. Toronto's _____ Shack

35. _____ Tocchet

38. Dismissed or _____ from the team

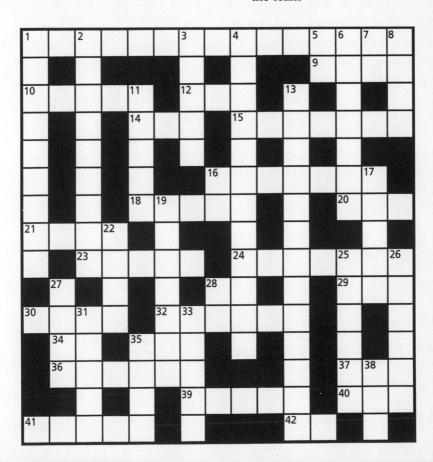

# 2
# TRUE BLUE

In 1999–2000, Philadelphia's rookie goalie Brian Boucher finished with a league-leading 1.91 goals-against average in 35 games. The last time a rookie netminder appeared in at least 25 games with an average under 2.00 was almost a half-century earlier, in 1950–51, when Toronto's Al Rollins (1.77 in 40 games) and Terry Sawchuk of Detroit (1.99 in 70 games) did it. "It's exciting," Boucher said. "It's a team statistic and I think the guys realized it in these last couple of games because they played really hard for me. Fifty years is a long time, and you only get one shot at being a rookie." In this chapter we have more team stats for the true blue.

(*Answers are on page 25*)

**2.1**  Based on their $61-million payroll—the highest in hockey history—how much did it cost the New York Rangers for each of their wins in 1999–2000?
A. $500,000 per win
B. $1 million per win
C. $1.5 million per win
D. $2 million per win

**2.2**  What is the most number of man-games lost by an NHL team in a season?
A. Less than 400 man-games
B. Between 400 and 500 man-games
C. Between 500 and 600 man-games
D. More than 600 man-games

**2.3**   In what year did the Philadelphia Flyers play their first game
without a penalty? (The Flyers entered the NHL in 1967.)
A. 1969
B. 1979
C. 1989
D. 1999

**2.4**   Which NHL team produced the first lineup with five 30-goal
scorers in one season?
A. The Chicago Blackhawks
B. The Boston Bruins
C. The Edmonton Oilers
D. The Montreal Canadiens

**2.5**   Which is the only Edmonton Oilers team to finish a road trip
of at least five games undefeated?
A. The Wayne Gretzky-led Oilers of the 1980s
B. The Mark Messier-led Oilers of the 1990s
C. The Jason Arnott-led Oilers of the 1990s
D. The Doug Weight-led Oilers of the late 1990s

**2.6**   Which NHL team has gone the longest without icing an NHL
scoring champion?
A. The Toronto Maple Leafs
B. The Detroit Red Wings
C. The New York Rangers
D. The Chicago Blackhawks

**2.7**   How many NHL teams did ironman Doug Jarvis play with to
establish his record 964-game streak over 12 seasons?
A. One team
B. Three teams
C. Five teams
D. Seven teams

**2.8** Against which team did the legendary Maurice Richard score most of his *milestone* goals, including the NHL's first 500th?

A. The Toronto Maple Leafs
B. The Chicago Blackhawks
C. The Detroit Red Wings
D. The New York Rangers

**2.9** If the individual record for the NHL's fastest hat trick is 21 seconds, what is the team record for three goals?

A. 16 seconds
B. 18 seconds
C. 20 seconds
D. 21 seconds

**2.10** How many of the Florida Panthers' team records did Pavel Bure break in 1999–2000?

A. Three records
B. Five records
C. Seven records
D. 21 records

**2.11** Who scored the most points for the New York Rangers in one season?

A. Jean Ratelle in 1971–72
B. Mike Rogers in 1981–82
C. Bernie Nicholls in 1989–90
D. Mark Messier in 1991–92

**2.12** Which NHL team began drinking a pink-coloured health-food drink called Endurox R4, after games, during the 1999–2000 season?
A. The Florida Panthers
B. The Buffalo Sabres
C. The Colorado Avalanche
D. The Los Angeles Kings

**2.13** Which Original Six team was saddled with "Muldoon's Curse"?
A. The Toronto Maple Leafs
B. The Boston Bruins
C. The Chicago Blackhawks
D. The Montreal Canadiens

**2.14** Prior to two NHL teams moving to different cities in 1976–77, when was the last time a franchise changed towns?
A. During the 1930s
B. During the 1940s
C. During the 1950s
D. During the 1960s

**2.15** Who is the only player to record 20-goal seasons with six different NHL teams?
A. Eddie Shack
B. Ray Sheppard
C. Dino Ciccarelli
D. Bernie Nicholls

**2.16** Which NHL team in 1999–2000 tied a 16-year-old league record for most consecutive road wins in a season?
A. The Buffalo Sabres
B. The New Jersey Devils
C. The Ottawa Senators
D. The St. Louis Blues

**2.17** In 1999–2000, how many NHL teams had no players wearing face shields?

    A. None, every team had at least one player wearing a shield

    B. Only one team

    C. Three teams

    D. Five teams

**2.18** With how many different teams did Wayne Gretzky win the Lady Byng Trophy as the league's most gentlemanly player?

    A. One team, Edmonton

    B. Two teams, Edmonton and Los Angeles

    C. Two teams, Edmonton and New York

    D. Three teams, Edmonton, Los Angeles and New York

**2.19** Which regular-playing Ottawa Senators skater wore the highest jersey number in 1999–2000?

    A. Radek Bonk

    B. Marian Hossa

    C. Joe Juneau

    D. Wade Redden

**2.20** In the NHL's first season of four-on-four play in regular-season overtime (where losing teams earned a point), how many teams concluded the season without earning a point for losing?

    A. Every team earned at least one point for losing in overtime

    B. Only one team

    C. Four teams

    D. Eight teams

**2.21** How many individual owners did the Edmonton Oilers franchise have in 1999–2000?

    A. Only one owner

    B. Two owners

    C. 10 owners

    D. More than 30 owners

**2.22** Which NHL team recorded the most wins in one decade of the 20th century?

A. The Boston Bruins of the 1930s

B. The Montreal Canadiens of the 1970s

C. The Edmonton Oilers of the 1980s

D. The Detroit Red Wings of the 1990s

# TRUE BLUE
## Answers

**2.1** **D. $2 million per win**

There is no better proof that money doesn't always buy success than the 1999–2000 New York Rangers. With the NHL's highest payroll in history—$61,194,011 (all figures in U.S. dollars)—the Rangers finished 23rd overall with a 29–41–15 record. Every victory cost the team $2.11 million; and each of their 218 goals was worth $280,706. The best bargain was the Ottawa Senators, who, with the 23rd-highest payroll, spent $24.887 million and finished 10th overall in the league. The first-place St. Louis Blues had the 12th biggest payroll: $34,630,019.

**2.2** **C. Between 500 and 600 man-games**

In 1998–99 the Washington Capitals lost 511 man-games due to injuries, the unofficial NHL record for games missed during a season. Amazingly, this mark was surpassed in 1999–2000 by the Montreal Canadiens, a team so injury-prone that by midseason seven regulars had missed at least 20 games, and 21 starters were sidelined for at least one game. The most serious injuries occurred to Brian Savage (two fractured vertebrae in the neck) and Trent McCleary (fractured larynx and collapsed lung). Savage missed 44 games after being hit cleanly by the Kings' Ian Laperrière; McCleary's injury was life-threatening, a slap shot to the throat. Only one Hab regular, Patrick Poulin, managed to stay healthy for all 82 games. The Canadiens lost 536 man-games at a cost of U.S.$9.5 million (a good chunk of the $32-million player budget). "There came a point in the season where it became a joke, because guys were going down every game," said Savage. "It was never a shock. We'd lose another guy and just keep going." The 1998–99 Capitals finished with a 31–45–6 record; the Canadiens were 35–38–9.

## 2.3   B.   1979
It's no surprise that the Flyers led the NHL in team penalty minutes from 1971 to 1982. Built in the Fred Shero mould of success through intimidation, Philadelphia bullied its way through the league to capture its first Stanley Cup in 1974 on the strength of a league-high 1,750 minutes in box time. The next most penalized team, the St. Louis Blues, had 34 per cent fewer penalties, just 1,147 minutes. That early Cup success defined the Flyers franchise of the future. The club's first penalty-free game came 12 years after it entered the NHL, on March 18, 1979, in a 5–3 win over the same Blues. Apparently, the boys were on their best behaviour after setting the league record for most penalty minutes (by a team in one period) a week earlier. In that March 11 game Philadelphia earned 188 minutes on four minors, eight majors, six 10-minute misconducts and eight game misconducts in the first period against Los Angeles.

## 2.4   A.   The Chicago Blackhawks
In 1968–69 Chicago's offensive powerhouse scored 280 goals, second only to Bobby Orr's Boston Bruins (303 goals). The scoring machine was sparked by Stan Mikita, Eric Nesterenko, Dennis Hull and Kenny Wharram, who each scored exactly 30 goals, while Bobby Hull established an NHL record 58 goals. The Blackhawks, however, were less successful at winning. Although Chicago became the first NHL club to ice five 30-goal scorers in one season, the club finished last in the tough East Division.

**2.5**  **D.  The Doug Weight-led Oilers of the late 1990s**
In one category, the 1999–2000 Oilers outperformed every other Edmonton team before them, even Wayne Gretzky's dynasty teams of the 1980s. Edmonton, who had never gone without a loss in a road trip of five games or more, went 3–0–2 between February 7 and 15, 2000. It was the first time in 47 road trips of at least five games (since joining the NHL in 1979) that the Oilers finished undefeated. "It's pretty amazing for us to do something that [no one has] ever done," said captain Doug Weight.

**2.6**  **A.  The Toronto Maple Leafs**
It has been more than half a century (and counting) since Toronto produced an NHL scoring leader. The last Leaf scoring champion was Gord Drillon, who led the league with 52 points in 1937–38. New York fans have been watching and waiting almost as long. New York hasn't seen a Ranger win the crown since 1941–42, when Bryan Hextall Sr. scored 56 points.

**2.7**  **B.  Three teams**
Jarvis, the NHL's ironman, never missed a game between 1975 and 1987. He played seven complete seasons with Montreal (560 games), three-and-a-half complete seasons with Washington (265 games) and almost two full seasons with Hartford (139 games) before packing it in just two games into the 1987–88 schedule. Jarvis only scored 139 goals in that span, but the defensive specialist didn't miss a game in a dozen years. In 1986–87, he broke Garry Unger's ironman streak of 914 games and won the Masterton Trophy for dedication to hockey.

**2.8**  **B.  The Chicago Blackhawks**
Richard scored his 500th goal on October 19, 1957, in a 3–1 win against the Blackhawks, the same club that the Rocket scored his 100th, 200th and 400th goals against. Chicago also fell victim to Richard's 325th, the historic marker which moved him past league leader Nels Stewart.

**2.9  C.  20 seconds**

Chicago's Bill Mosienko bagged the NHL's quickest hat trick in 21 seconds (on March 23, 1952), just one second off the team mark later set by Boston in 1971. The Bruins' three-goal outburst came in 20 seconds, as Johnny Bucyk at 4:50, Ed Westfall at 5:02 and Ted Green at 5:10 scored in rapid succession during the third period of an 8–3 win over Vancouver on February 25, 1971. More recently, Washington missed the mark by one second with a team hat trick in 21 seconds, on November 23, 1990.

**2.10  D.  21 records**

Floridians haven't seen a hometown athlete like Pavel Bure since Dan Marino at his height in the NFL. In short order, Bure erased 21 team records in almost every category for goals, including goals in a period (3), in a game (4), in a season (58), game winners (14), empty netters (9), even-strength (45), third-period goals (29), season hat tricks (4) and career hat tricks (6). Bure also smashed or tied Panther records for points in a period (3), points in a game (4), points per game (1.3), even-strength points (72), season points (94), most shots in a game (11) and in a season (360), and the best plus/minus (plus-25). He set another four club records in scoring streaks, including for goals (five games), game-winning goals (three games), assists (seven games) and, finally, points (13 games).

**2.11  A.  Jean Ratelle in 1971–72**

In New York history, six Rangers have scored 100 points or more in one season. And although Bernie Nicholls, Mark Messier and Brian Leetch rank high in this All-Star pack, none top Ratelle, who became New York's first century man in 1971–72, when he recorded 109 points. More impressive, he shattered the single-season team mark by 21 points while playing in only 63 games after suffering a broken ankle on March 1. Bernie Nicholls had a 112-point year in 1989–90, but his numbers were split between Los Angeles (75 points) and New York (37).

**2.12 C. The Colorado Avalanche**
Game after game the Avalanche gulp down a drink that looks like Pepto-Bismol and smells like Nestlé Strawberry Quik. Endurox R4 is a nutritional supplement for improving recovery from strenuous physical activity and reducing muscle stress. "They say to drink it, so I drink," commented Avalanche right-winger Milan Hejduk to the *National Post*. "I don't know much about what it does, but they say it's good for you."

**2.13 C. The Chicago Blackhawks**
"Muldoon's Curse" dates back to Chicago's inaugural season when Pete Muldoon, the Hawks' first head coach, cursed the team—vowing it would never finish first—after he was sent packing in 1927. Although the story (and the curse) was a fabrication of hockey writer Jim Coleman, Chicago didn't finish in first place until 1966–67, 40 years later. Hawk forward Stan Mikita mocked: "Is the champagne cold? It ought to be—it's been on ice for 40 years."

**2.14 A. During the 1930s**
Prior to Kansas City moving to Colorado and California to Cleveland in 1976–77, the last time an NHL franchise changed locations was in 1934–35, when the old Ottawa Senators were reincarnated as the Eagles in St. Louis. Like the Colorado Rockies and Cleveland Barons in the 1970s, the move didn't help the Eagles. All three teams finished last in their divisions.

**2.15 B. Ray Sheppard**
The quintessential journeyman, Sheppard rang up 25 goals for the Carolina Hurricanes in 1998–99, giving him 20-goal seasons with a record six NHL teams. He had already reached the 20-goal mark with the Buffalo Sabres, New York Rangers, Detroit Red Wings, San Jose Sharks and Florida Panthers.

**2.16  D.  The St. Louis Blues**
The Blues were the surprise story of 1999–2000. They finished first overall, partly on the strength of a 10-game road-winning streak in February that tied the Buffalo Sabres' old road record of 1983–84. "No matter who the opponent is, we play the same style," coach Joel Quenneville told the *St. Louis Post-Dispatch*. That consistent style of play had everyone contributing. Nine players scored winning goals (Lubos Bartecko scored two), 15 players scored at least once and 23 players had at least one point during the streak. Goalie Roman Turek, the model of consistency, went 9–0–1 with a 1.38 goals-against average and a .940 save percentage. The Blues' defense restricted the opposition to 23 shots per game, and the club killed off 60 of 66 power plays. Unfortunately, the bubble burst in the 11th away game, when St. Louis tied Florida 1–1 on March 4.

**2.17  B.  Only one team**
In the wake of the horrific eye injury of Toronto's Bryan Berard in March 2000, the *Hockey News* conducted a team-by-team survey of visor use in the NHL. The Edmonton Oilers were the only team in 1999–2000 without a player wearing a face shield. St. Louis had just one visor wearer, Pierre Turgeon. Two teams— the New Jersey Devils and the New York Rangers—led the pack with nine visor-wearing players. Among 644 NHLers in 1999– 2000, only 133 players, or 21 per cent, wore visors. Further, almost half (49 per cent), or 65, of those visor wearers were European, a group that represents only 28 per cent of the NHL population. More than one-third of Europlayers donned visors compared to about one-seventh of North Americans.

**2.18  D.  Three teams, Edmonton, Los Angeles and New York**
Gretzky won five Lady Byngs on three different teams during his 20-year NHL career: one with Edmonton, in 1980; three with Los Angeles, in 1991, 1992 and 1994; and one in New York, in 1999. Only Rangers great Frank Boucher has been named most

gentlemanly player more often than the Great One. Boucher was honoured seven times during the 1920s and 1930s.

**2.19  C.  Joe Juneau**

After Pierre Gauthier took over as Ottawa general manager in the mid-1990s, high sweater numbers went the same way as under-achiever Alexandre Daigle: flushed from the Senators' roster. Gauthier believed that allowing a few players higher digits affected team unity, so everyone was forced to wear numbers in the lower stratosphere. With Gauthier gone, the club rule seems to be softening, but only in a few cases. Goalie Patrick Lalime got No. 40, and Joe Juneau No. 28 before his request for No. 39 was approved late in 1999–2000. Juneau was No. 9 throughout his days in youth hockey and has always had that digit in the NHL. He wore No. 90 in Washington and Buffalo. "You look at your jersey, and for some reason I just feel better about it. I always felt very bad about No. 28. Sometimes I felt like a defenseman with that number."

**2.20  B.  Only one team**

First some history. In 1998–99, the American Hockey League experimented with four-on-four play to determine if the strategy would reduce ties. In fact, the play was not only exciting, but 61 per cent of overtime games were decided, as opposed to just 27 per cent of NHL overtime games (where each team still played five aside). Coupled with four-on-four as an incentive to win, teams were assured one point, even if they lost in the extra period. In the 1999–2000 season, every NHL team except Carolina earned one point for losing in overtime. In all, 114 points were awarded to 27 teams in the regulation ties column (fourth digit after team wins, losses and ties). The new regulation ties column helped a few clubs improve points-wise over the previous season. Toronto, with an identical record of 45–30–7 in 1998–99 and 1999–2000, increased from 97 points to 100 points because of three regulation ties. Edmonton and Vancouver earned eight points, the most among NHL teams, from regulation ties. The Oilers finished 1999–2000 with 88 points, 10 points ahead of 1998–99's 78-point mark, even though they had one less win in 1999–2000 than in 1998–99 (33).

## THE 20TH CENTURY'S TOP WINNING NHL TEAMS*

|  | W | L | T | Pct. |
|---|---|---|---|---|
| The 1990s |  |  |  |  |
| Detroit Red Wings | 429 | 252 | 99 | .613 |
| The 1980s |  |  |  |  |
| Edmonton Oilers | 458 | 243 | 104 | .634 |
| The 1970s |  |  |  |  |
| Montreal Canadiens | 501 | 160 | 130 | .716 |
| The 1960s |  |  |  |  |
| Montreal Canadiens | 378 | 204 | 128 | .623 |
| The 1950s |  |  |  |  |
| Montreal Canadiens | 363 | 210 | 128 | .609 |
| The 1940s |  |  |  |  |
| Detroit Red Wings | 260 | 193 | 84 | .562 |
| The 1930s |  |  |  |  |
| Boston Bruins | 259 | 154 | 63 | .610 |
| The 1920s |  |  |  |  |
| Ottawa Senators | 186 | 108 | 39 | .617 |
| The 1910s |  |  |  |  |
| Montreal Canadiens | 24 | 19 | 0 | .558 |

*Statistics (by decade) from the National Post

**2.21** D. **More than 30 owners**

The Edmonton Investors Group may have saved the NHL franchise from moving out of Alberta, but the 37-member company of Oilers owners hasn't impressed General Manager Glen Sather. On working for 37 owners, Sather said, "This has been an ongoing problem since day one. I hate to say this, but [his former assistant] Doug Risebrough was right. He said 'It won't work.' One of these guys one time said it was no different running a gas station than running a hockey team. Can you believe that?" The unwieldy front-office situation led to Sather leaving the Oilers at the end of the 1999–2000 season.

**2.22** B. **The Montreal Canadiens of the 1970s**

Managed by Sam Pollock, hockey's most astute player appraiser and deal maker, and led by Scotty Bowman, the coach who has won the most NHL games, the Montreal Canadiens compiled 501 wins during the 1970s. They lost just 160 games and tied 130 for a sparkling .716 record in the 10-year span. No other team in NHL history recorded better win-loss-tie numbers in any decade during the 20th century.

# Game 2
# STRANGE STARTS

Before Brett Hull became the NHL's leading goal scorer of the 1990s with St. Louis and Dallas, he played 57 games for another team that traded him to the Blues. So which unlucky club gave up on Brett? The answer is included below. Match the player with his first-year club.

(*Solutions are on page 120*)

### Part 1

1. _____ St. Louis' Brett Hull          A. New York Rangers

2. _____ Boston's Cam Neely            B. Montreal Canadiens

3. _____ The Flyers' Reggie Leach       C. Detroit Red Wings

4. _____ Washington's Adam Oates        D. Calgary Flames

5. _____ Chicago's Tony Esposito        E. Toronto Maple Leafs

6. _____ Boston's Rick Middleton        F. Boston Bruins

7. _____ Winnipeg's Randy Carlyle       G. Vancouver Canucks

### Part 2

1. _____ Buffalo's Dominik Hasek        A. Quebec Nordiques

2. _____ Toronto's Eddie Shack          B. Chicago Blackhawks

3. _____ Pittsburgh's Rick Kehoe        C. Detroit Red Wings

4. _____ The Flyers' Bernie Parent      D. Winnipeg Jets

5. _____ Toronto's Mats Sundin          E. Toronto Maple Leafs

6. _____ Anaheim's Teemu Selanne        F. Boston Bruins

7. _____ The Kings' Marcel Dionne       G. New York Rangers

# 3
# MAKING HISTORY

The year 2000 gave the media plenty of opportunity to reflect on the best of the last 100 years. Michael Jordan topped the ESPN list of the century's best athletes; Babe Ruth was the best according to the Associated Press. And on both the top-100 lists, Wayne Gretzky was voted the world's best hockey player, and was the fifth athlete listed. The Great One was also named by *Sports Illustrated* as the hockey player of the century. *SI*'s coveted choice for its number one "moment in sports" went to hockey's "Miracle on Ice" team, the overachieving U.S. squad that won the gold at the 1980 Olympics. Canadian editors and broadcasters voted 1972's Team Canada the number one team of the century, followed by the 1980s Edmonton Oilers dynasty and the 1950s Montreal Canadiens dynasty. In this chapter we reflect on some other big, and small, milestones in hockey history.

*(Answers are on page 40)*

**3.1** In what decade did team logos first appear on NHL pucks?
   A. In the 1940s
   B. In the 1950s
   C. In the 1960s
   D. In the 1970s

**3.2** How long did it take the Government of Canada to revoke its subsidy package to Canadian-based NHL teams in January 2000?
   A. Four hours
   B. Four days
   C. Four weeks
   D. Four months

**3.3**   The NHL held benefit All-Star games to honour which old-timers during the 1930s?

A.   Toronto's Ace Bailey

B.   Montreal's Howie Morenz

C.   Montreal's Babe Siebert

D.   All of the above

**3.4**   In what season did a Soviet-trained player first play in the NHL?

A. 1979–80

B. 1982–83

C. 1985–86

D. 1988–89

**3.5**   What 1963 incident led NHL arenas to install separate penalty boxes for each team?

A.   A sell-out crowd

B.   A peanut vendor's heart attack

C.   A player fight

D.   A coach's dismissal

**3.6**   In what year were aluminum sticks approved for NHL use?

A.   1962

B.   1972

C.   1982

D.   1992

**3.7**   Who was the first NHL head coach to hire an assistant coach?

A.   Fred Shero of the Philadelphia Flyers

B.   Scotty Bowman of the Montreal Canadiens

C.   Glen Sather of the Edmonton Oilers

D.   Al Arbour of the New York Islanders

**3.8** In what year was the first empty-net goal scored in the NHL?
A. 1933
B. 1943
C. 1953
D. 1963

**3.9** How many players were involved in the largest trade in NHL history?
A. Six players
B. Eight players
C. 10 players
D. 12 players

**3.10** During Wayne Gretzky's record-breaking performance in 1982–83, he earned more assists (125) than anyone had points. Prior to Gretzky, when was the last time another NHLer accomplished the feat?
A. During the 1940s
B. During the 1950s
C. During the 1960s
D. It had never happened before

**3.11** In what year did the NHL introduce the five-minute overtime period during the regular season?
A. 1979–80
B. 1981–82
C. 1983–84
D. 1985–86

**3.12** Who was the first NHLer to score a goal during the new four-on-four overtime format in 1999–2000?
A. Dallas' Brett Hull
B. Montreal's Brian Savage
C. Calgary's Valeri Bure
D. San Jose's Mike Ricci

**3.13** Who scored the most goals during the 1990s?
A. Wayne Gretzky
B. Jaromir Jagr
C. Brett Hull
D. Steve Yzerman

**3.14** After Wayne Gretzky, who scored the most assists during the 1990s?
A. Doug Gilmour
B. Adam Oates
C. Ron Francis
D. Joe Sakic

**3.15** Wayne Gretzky scored 940 points during the 1990s. How many fewer points did runner-up Jaromir Jagr score during the decade?
A. 12 points fewer
B. 32 points fewer
C. 62 points fewer
D. 92 points fewer

**3.16** In which decade did player numbers first appear on hockey jerseys?
A. The 1910s
B. The 1920s
C. The 1930s
D. The 1940s

**3.17** NHL rookie of the year winners are not always first-round draft picks. Which Calder Trophy recipient was not picked until the 14th round of the Entry Draft (241st overall)?
A. Gary Suter
B. Steve Larmer
C. Luc Robitaille
D. Sergei Makarov

**3.18** What was the age of the NHL's oldest MVP winner?
(Name him.)
- A. 30 years old
- B. 32 years old
- C. 34 years old
- D. 36 years old

**3.19** The record for most number of goals scored in one season by siblings is held by the six Sutter brothers. What is their best season total?
- A. 98 goals
- B. 118 goals
- C. 138 goals
- D. 158 goals

**3.20** After centring the NHL's first All-Star team for six successive years between 1968–69 and 1973–74, Phil Esposito was replaced by which player at centre in All-Star voting in 1974–75?
- A. Buffalo's Gilbert Perreault
- B. Philadelphia's Bobby Clarke
- C. Detroit's Marcel Dionne
- D. New York's Jean Ratelle

**3.21** In 1999 the NHL created the Maurice Richard Trophy, an annual award to honour the NHL's leading goal scorer. How many times would Richard have won the trophy if it had existed in his day?
- A. Once
- B. Three times
- C. Five times
- D. Seven times

# MAKING HISTORY
## Answers

**3.1**  **B.  In the 1950s**
The simple black puck has been decorated in many ways since it was first introduced during the late 1800s. Originally, it was a square-shaped piece of wood. Then, in 1886, the rubber puck became hockey's official disk (three inches in diameter, one inch thick and weighing six ounces); it remained a basic black until the early 1950s, when team logos began to grace its smooth surface. The World Hockey Association, the NHL's rival league in the 1970s, then upped the ante and introduced red, blue and other coloured pucks into their game. But the idea was soon scrapped, as were two later innovations: the Minnesota North Stars' so-called "fire puck" (used only in practices), and its successor, the loathsome foxtrax puck, which emitted streaks of red-and-blue light to help the American TV audience follow the play.

**3.2**  **B.  Four days**
Canadian-based NHL teams have long been seeking government monies and tax breaks to better balance the franchise economies between themselves and rich American teams. Finally, on January 18, 2000, Canadian industry minister John Manley announced a federal government aid package to help cash-strapped Canadian teams. The plan (with strings attached) included $20 million per year until 2004. But only four days later, Manley stepped before the cameras and declared the unprecedented deal "dead," after a wave of negative reaction from politicians, the media and the public.

**3.3**  **D.  All of the above**
Prior to the first official All-Star game in 1947, the NHL held three charity All-Star games during the 1930s. In 1934, the Maple Leafs beat a group of NHL All-Stars 7–3 in the Ace Bailey

Benefit Game. Bailey, a star scorer, suffered a career-ending head injury months earlier. Then, in 1937, after the tragic death of Howie Morenz, another team of NHL stars defeated the Montreal Canadiens 6–5 in the Howie Morenz Memorial Game. Two years later, a third NHL benefit game was played in honour of Babe Siebert, a 14-year veteran who died in the summer of 1939 before beginning coaching duties with Montreal. The NHL stars beat the Canadiens 5–2.

**3.4   B.  1982–83**
In 1982–83, Viktor Nechayev appeared in three games with the Los Angeles Kings, scoring one goal. Picked 132nd overall by the Kings in the seventh round of the 1982 Entry Draft, the Soviet forward had immigrated to the U.S. after marrying an American nurse he met in Russia. Nechayev was demoted to the minors after his brief NHL stint, and eventually released. He played another year in Germany before retiring. The second Soviet to play in the NHL was Sergei Priakin, who joined the Calgary Flames late in the 1988–89 season.

**3.5   C.  A player fight**
Until the mid-1960s, NHL arenas had one penalty box for both teams. That changed soon after a fight between Montreal's Terry Harper and Toronto's Bob Pulford at Maple Leaf Gardens in Toronto, November 8, 1963. Pulford and Harper, already thrown off the ice for fisticuffs, couldn't contain themselves at such close striking distance and resumed their battle in the box. Soon, teams installed separate penalty box doors and, eventually, separate home and visitor penalty boxes.

**3.6   C.  1982**
Long before Wayne Gretzky took his aluminum-shafted Easton and turned the hockey world on edge, Brad Park was quietly experimenting with the game's first aluminum stick. The blade was wood but it slid into a metal shaft that had been developed

by the famous Quebec stickmaker, Sher-Wood. Park began using it during practices as early as 1979, then, after league approval, regularly in 1982. At that time only a few other players, including Stan Johnathan and Dave Christian, followed Park's lead and abandoned the traditional wooden stick.

**3.7 A. Fred Shero of the Philadelphia Flyers**
Shero introduced the concept of the assistant coach to the NHL, when he hired Mike Nykoluk (and later Barry Ashbee) to help run the Flyers in 1972. Today, assistant coaches are as common (and essential) behind the bench as trainers.

**3.8 B. 1943**
Clint Smith, of the Chicago Blackhawks, scored the NHL's first empty-netter at 19:12 of the third period in a game versus the Boston Bruins, November 11, 1943. Smith put the puck in the vacant cage after the Bruins' coach, Art Ross, pulled goalie Bert Gardiner for an extra attacker in the 5–4 game. Ross was the first NHL coach to try such a strategy and the first to get burnt by it. The goal gave the Hawks a 6–4 victory over Boston.

**3.9 C. 10 players**
The biggest trade in NHL history sent 10 players to two different teams. Doug Gilmour was the prize catch when Calgary sent him, along with Ric Nattress, Jamie Macoun, Rick Wamsley and Kent Manderville, to Toronto, on January 2, 1992, in exchange for Gary Leeman, Craig Berube, Jeff Reese, Alexander Godynyuk and Michel Petit. The Maple Leafs got the nod in this deal, as Gilmour led Toronto to two semifinal finishes the next two seasons. It was the Leafs' best playoff performance in 25 years.

**3.10 A. During the 1940s**
Other than Wayne Gretzky, only one other player in NHL history finished a regular season with more assists than anyone else had points. He was Boston's Bill Cowley, who, in 1940–41, accumu-

lated 45 assists (one point better than five runners-up in the NHL scoring race). Like Gretzky, Cowley was a skilled playmaker who could thread the puck to his wingers through a forest of sticks. His career assist total (353) almost doubled his goal output (195). During his 13-year Hall of Fame career he won two Hart Trophies as league MVP, four First All-Star Team selections, two Stanley Cups and an Art Ross Trophy as scoring champion in 1940–41. Cowley was inducted into the Hall of Fame in 1969.

**3.11  C.  1983–84**
After a 41-year break, the NHL added a five-minute sudden-death overtime period to regular-season games that ended in ties. In the first season, 1983–84, 54 of 140 games were decided in the extra frame. New York Islanders general manager Bill Torrey compared the brief period to "15 seconds of sex. If we are going to have overtime," said Torrey, "let's play to a finish."

**3.12  D.  San Jose's Mike Ricci**
The first player to register an overtime goal in the NHL's inaugural season of four-on-four was Mike Ricci, who scored the historic marker in a four-on-three power play against Edmonton on October 7, 1999. The format's fast-paced play increased scoring chances, but, again, hot goaltending prevailed: 13 of the first 15 overtime games in 1999–2000 finished in a tie; goalies stopped 90 of 92 overtime shots. The first scorer in true four-on-four play (with neither team being penalized) was Valeri Bure, in a 3–2 overtime win October 13, 1999.

**3.13  C.  Brett Hull**
The Golden Brett led all NHL snipers in goals during the 1990s. He was just six goals shy of reaching the 500-goals-in-a-decade plateau, scoring 494 times between 1990 and 2000. His two final goals of the decade gave Dallas the tying and winning goals in a 5–4 victory over Anaheim on December 31, 1999. "It's been a great decade. I couldn't have capped it any better," said

Hull. For the record, only two players amassed 500 goals in a calendar decade. Phil Esposito scored 518 in the 1970s; Wayne Gretzky notched 627 goals in the 1980s.

---

## TOP SNIPERS OF THE 1990s[*]

| Player | Team | Goals |
|---|---|---|
| Brett Hull | St. Louis/Dallas | 494 |
| Jaromir Jagr | Pittsburgh | 376 |
| Brendan Shanahan | NJ/St.L/Hart/Det | 369 |
| Luc Robitaille | LA/Pit/NYR/LA | 357 |
| Theoren Fleury | Cal/Col/NYR | 355 |
| Steve Yzerman | Detroit | 352 |

*Based on a calendar decade*

---

**3.14 B. Adam Oates**

After Wayne Gretzky's 702 helpers, the next-best assist total of the 1990s belongs to Adam Oates. On his way to collecting 674 assists, Oates helped the likes of Brett Hull, Cam Neely and Peter Bondra to 50-goal years throughout the decade.

---

## ASSIST LEADERS OF THE 1990s[*]

| Player | Team | Assists |
|---|---|---|
| Wayne Gretzky | LA/St.L/NYR | 702 |
| Adam Oates | St.L/Bos/Wash | 674 |
| Ron Francis | Hart/Pit/Car | 592 |
| Doug Gilmour | Cal/Tor/NJ/Chi | 560 |
| Joe Sakic | Quebec/Colorado | 557 |
| Jaromir Jagr | Pittsburgh | 552 |

*Based on a calendar decade*

---

## 3.15  A.  12 points fewer

When Wayne Gretzky retired in 1999, he said that he was passing the torch to Jaromir Jagr. Based on the 12-point difference in point totals during the 1990s, Jagr might have already been carrying the torch for some time before Gretzky's retirement.

---

### TOP POINT EARNERS OF THE 1990S*

| Player | Team | Points |
|---|---|---|
| Wayne Gretzky | LA/St.L/NYR | 940 |
| Jaromir Jagr | Pittsburgh | 928 |
| Adam Oates | St.L/Bos/Wash | 902 |
| Steve Yzerman | Detroit | 896 |
| Joe Sakic | Quebec/Colorado | 895 |
| Brett Hull | St. Louis/Dallas | 873 |

*Based on a calendar decade

---

## 3.16  A.  The 1910s

Based on what researchers now know, the first numbers on athletic uniforms appeared in 1908 on a few American college football teams. The practice of hockey numbers dates to 1914, when the Pacific Coast Hockey Association and the Montreal Wanderers of the National Hockey Association began using numbers one through 15 on team jerseys. In that era, much higher numbers were usually reserved for irregulars and backup goalies.

## 3.17  D.  Sergei Makarov

There are always a few hidden gems each draft year; some even turn into Calder Trophy winners. Larmer (120th), Robitalle (171st) and Suter (180th), all overlooked by NHL scouts in their drafts, are prime examples of underrated juniors who later flourished as NHLers. But Makarov was different. When the Calgary Flames selected him in the last round (241st overall) at the 1983

Entry Draft, he was playing with the Central Army team in the Soviet Union's elite league. Makarov was already a multiple winner of the Izvestia Trophy as the U.S.S.R.'s leading scorer, an eight-time member of the U.S.S.R. All-Star team and the U.S.S.R.'s player of the year in 1980, 1985 and 1989. His talent wasn't in question; it was Soviet politics that left many in doubt. But Calgary figured that Makarov was at least worth wasting a last-round pick. Six years later when the Soviets eased their grip and a few veterans, including Makarov, trickled into the NHL, Calgary had their man. At 31 years old, the 12-year international veteran of Olympic and world championships scored 86 points in the NHL and won the Calder Trophy. He is the lowest draft pick (and the oldest player) to win the Calder as rookie of the year.

**3.18  D.  36 years old**
Although the average age of most Hart winners is 28, a few players have won an MVP title in their thirties. Dominik Hasek was 33 when he captured his second Hart in 1998. Eddie Shore of Boston and Detroit's Gordie Howe were both 35 when they won in 1938 and 1963. The eldest MVP is Herb Gardiner, who joined the NHL at age 35 after playing for the Calgary Tigers in the rival Western Canada Hockey League. The big blueliner was awarded the Hart at age 36, after leading Montreal to the best defensive record in the league in 1926–27. Born May 8, 1891, Gardiner is one of only two MVPs born in the 19th century (the other is Frank Nighbor). The youngest Hart winner is Wayne Gretzky (for his win at age 19).

**3.19  C.  138 goals**
No family in NHL history can match the Sutters, either in number of players or total goals scored. During the 1980s, when Brent, Brian, Darryl, Duane, Rich and Ron were all playing, they amassed a league-high 138 goals—in both 1983–84 and 1984–85. The next-best season total for brothers belongs to the

three Stastnys—Peter, Anton and Marian—who combined for a 115-goal count in 1982–83. Between 1976–77 and 1999–2000, the Sutters scored a combined 1,324 goals, another league standard.

**3.20  B.  Philadelphia's Bobby Clarke**

Esposito's domination as centre on the First All-Star Team ended after six seasons in 1974–75, when Bobby Clarke was named the NHL's top pivot. Clarke, the captain and inspirational leader of the Stanley Cup-winning Philadelphia Flyers, posted the second 100-point season of his career with 116 points, 11 less than Esposito's 127.

**3.21  C.  Five times**

Maurice Richard led the NHL in goal scoring in 1944–45, 1946–47, 1949–50, 1953–54 and 1954–55. Richard's five goal-scoring titles tied him with Charlie Conacher for top spot in the category. The mark was later erased by Bobby Hull, who led the league in goal scoring a record seven times.

# Game 3

# AMERICAN OLYMPIANS

Which amateur U.S. Olympian went on to record the best NHL career? Unscramble the American Olympians' names below by placing each letter in the correct order in the boxes. (To help you, each name starts with the bolded letter.) Then, unscramble the letters in the circled boxes to spell out our mystery Olympian. The letters in the darkened circles are his initials.

*(Solutions are on page 120)*

T R **B** N O

L **C** O H I E S

V I **P** A L E C H

N A T O R **G** A

H U K K A C **T**

T C **L** E E H

A T E **I** F R A

48

# 4
# MARATHON MEN

Nobody logs more playing time than hockey's defenders. Goaltenders play entire games, and defensemen average more ice time than any other skaters. In fact, when the NHL released its list for average ice time in 1999–2000, the first 21 names were rearguards, among them Sergei Zubov, Derian Hatcher and Chris Pronger, who led the league with 30 minutes, 14 seconds per game. This chapter is devoted to the defensive workhorses of the NHL.

(*Answers are on page 54*)

4.1   According to New Jersey's Martin Brodeur, how many games does a great goaltender steal for his team during the course of a season?
A.  Three games
B.  Five games
C.  Seven games
D.  Nine games

4.2   How many games has defenseman Larry Murphy missed since he began playing NHL hockey in 1980–81?
A.  Less than 30 games
B.  Between 30 and 90 games
C.  Between 90 and 150 games
D.  More than 150 games

**4.3** Which goalie holds the mark for playing the most minutes in a season in which he also led the NHL in goals-against average?
A. Ed Belfour
B. Dominik Hasek
C. Bernie Parent
D. Jacques Plante

**4.4** Among the four Norris Trophy winners below, who was the oldest player to win the NHL's top defenseman award?
A. Al MacInnis
B. Rob Blake
C. Ray Bourque
D. Chris Chelios

**4.5** Defensive great Serge Savard scored just 106 goals in 1,040 career games, or one goal about every 10 games. What is the worst games-per-goal total among players with 1,000 NHL games?
A. About 12 games per goal
B. About 24 games per goal
C. About 36 games per goal
D. About 48 games per goal

**4.6** As of 1999–2000, how many NHL goalies have gone on to become head coaches in the league?
A. Eight goalies
B. 18 goalies
C. 28 goalies
D. 48 goalies

**4.7** What is the highest number of scoreless games in an NHL season in modern-day hockey?
   A. Two scoreless games
   B. Four scoreless games
   C. Six scoreless games
   D. Eight scoreless games

**4.8** Which two defensemen in 1998–99 passed Tim Horton's record of 1,446 regular-season games, the most of any NHL rearguard?
   A. Paul Coffey and Larry Murphy
   B. Larry Murphy and Ray Bourque
   C. Ray Bourque and Scott Stevens
   D. Scott Stevens and Craig Ludwig

**4.9** Who was the first NHL goalie to score a game-winning goal?
   A. Billy Smith
   B. Ron Hextall
   C. Chris Osgood
   D. Martin Brodeur

**4.10** Which Norris Trophy-winning defenseman was traded by his original team for an NHL penalty leader?
   A. Paul Coffey
   B. Bobby Orr
   C. Doug Harvey
   D. Chris Chelios

**4.11** In his last great season, 1974–75, Bobby Orr scored a league-leading 135 points to win the NHL scoring race. If runner-up Phil Esposito was eight points back with 127, how far back was the next-best defenseman? (Who was he?)
A. Less than 30 points back
B. Between 30 and 40 points back
C. Between 40 and 50 points back
D. More than 50 points back

**4.12** How long did Bobby Orr's 46-goal regular-season record for defensemen last?
A. One year
B. 11 years
C. 22 years
D. It has never been broken

**4.13** How many wins did goalie Michel Belhumeur post in the 35 games he appeared in with the Washington Capitals in 1974–75 (the year the Caps set so many NHL losing and winless team records)?
A. No wins
B. One win
C. Five wins
D. Nine wins

**4.14** In his last season in Boston, 1999–2000, Ray Bourque played with rookie goalie John Grahame. How was Grahame's father, Ron Grahame, connected to Bourque years earlier?
A. Ron Grahame was traded by Boston for Ray Bourque
B. Ron Grahame was Ray Bourque's first defense partner
C. Ron Grahame was Calder Trophy runner-up to Ray Bourque
D. Ron Grahame was Ray Bourque's first NHL coach

**4.15** In 1998–99, the NHL standardized the goaltender's catching glove to 50 inches. What did the league reduce or increase that measurement to the following season (1999–2000)?
A. 46 inches
B. 48 inches
C. 52 inches
D. 54 inches

**4.16** Which NHL defenseman blocked the most shots in 1998–99, the first year the league tracked the statistic?
A. Ray Bourque
B. Rob Blake
C. Brian Leetch
D. Ken Daneyko

**4.17** Toronto coach and former defenseman Pat Quinn played nine NHL seasons, but he is best remembered for delivering a crushing body check that knocked out which superstar?
A. Bobby Orr
B. Guy Lafleur
C. Bobby Clarke
D. Phil Esposito

**4.18** Which goalie with 250-plus games played had the best overall goals-against average during the 1990s?
A. Ed Belfour
B. Dominik Hasek
C. Martin Brodeur
D. Patrick Roy

**4.19** On February 2, 1977, Toronto's Ian Turnbull established the single-game goal record for NHL defensemen by scoring five times in a 9–1 win over Detroit. How many shots did Turnbull take to score those five goals?

A.  Five shots

B.  Seven shots

C.  Nine shots

D.  11 shots

**4.20** How many different sweater numbers has Chris Chelios worn during his playing days in Montreal, Chicago and Detroit?

A.  Only one, No. 7

B.  Two sweater numbers

C.  Three sweater numbers

D.  Four sweater numbers

**4.21** Which goalie holds the NHL record for most career wins, including playoffs?

A.  Jacques Plante

B.  Terry Sawchuk

C.  Grant Fuhr

D.  Patrick Roy

# MARATHON MEN
## Answers

**4.1**  **B.  Five games**
On being asked how many games a great goaltender steals in a season, Martin Brodeur humbly responded, "By myself, I probably steal up to five games that we have no business winning." Longtime Devils defenseman Ken Dayenko, asked the same question about Brodeur, thought his backstopper was a little conservative. "I think probably eight," said Dayenko.

**4.2  A.  Less than 30 games**

During the 1999–2000 season, 20-year man Larry Murphy slipped into runner-up position on the NHL's all-time games-played list, second only to the indomitable Gordie Howe. Murphy passed Wayne Gretzky, Johnny Bucyk and Alex Delvecchio to secure the number two spot with 1,558 games played, nine more than Detroit old-timer Delvecchio. Murphy has 207 games, or about three more seasons, to catch Howe. "Gordie's a few years away. If I'm still playing at that point, I'm sure he will come back and play again. I think it'll be impossible to catch him," Murphy told the *Detroit Free Press*. More impressive, in 1,558 games the 39-year-old rearguard has only missed 28 games.

**4.3  C.  Bernie Parent**

The Philadelphia Flyers' masked marvel logged 4,314 minutes between the pipes and posted a league-leading 1.89 goals-against average in 1973–74, the heaviest workload of a Vezina Trophy winner. Hasek ranks second among Vezina winners with 4,220 minutes of net time. Although Plante played every minute of every game for Montreal during his Vezina-winning season of 1961–62, the schedule was only 70 games, so his total was limited to 4,200 minutes.

**4.4  A.  Al MacInnis**

Winning the Norris Trophy as the league's top rearguard in 1999 didn't bring MacInnis newfound respect as one of the game's finest defensemen. That reputation had already been well-established during his distinguished 18-year career. So what took the St. Louis blueliner so long to garner the best D-man award? Overshadowed by the Bourques, Coffeys and Chelioses, MacInnis had twice been bridesmaid as the trophy's runner-up. When he finally won the Norris in 1998–99, he was almost 36, the most senior winner ever. MacInnis led all defensemen with 62 points and 314 shots on goal. Behind the blueline he was equally effective, ranking among the league leaders with a plus-33 rating.

**4.5    D.  About 48 games per goal**
In 17 seasons, Dallas' defensive defenseman Craig Ludwig scored just 38 goals in 1,256 games, or one goal every 33 games. Yet, in comparison to Brad Marsh, Ludwig is almost a sniper. Marsh is the least effective goal scorer among 1,000-game NHLers. The former rearguard scored just 23 times in 1,086 games, an average of 47.2 games for every goal.

**4.6    A.  Eight goalies**
If numbers mean anything, goalies make better TV colour analysts than head coaches; in today's NHL there are more retired netminders in front of the camera than behind the bench. In fact, the John Davidsons, Greg Millens and Brian Haywards far outnumber their brethren who coach. Incredibly, only eight goalies have ever gone on to coach in NHL history. Hugh Lehman coached 21 games in his last season of play, 1927–28; Emile Francis played 95 games during the late 1940s and early 1950s and later coached 778 games between 1963 and 1983; Roger Crozier laced up for 518 games and coached just one match (a loss) for Washington in 1981; Eddie Johnston backstopped 592 contests and coached 596 games; Bob Johnson worked the pipes in only 24 games but coached 480 games, including a Stanley Cup in Pittsburgh; Rogie Vachon played in 795 games and stood behind the bench as a substitute 10 times; Gerry Cheevers wore the pads 418 times and later coached his Bruins on 376 occasions; and Ron Low suited up for six teams and 382 games, then coached for 341 games (to date).

**4.7    C.  Six scoreless games**
The 1997–98 season produced a record 160 shutouts, including six 0–0 games, the most scoreless matches in an NHL season since 1935–36 (when NHL teams produced another six scoreless games).

The six score-free matchups in 1997–98 were San Jose-Toronto (November 4), Chicago-Edmonton (December 17), San Jose-Vancouver (December 18), Boston-Ottawa (January 1), Ottawa-Pittsburgh (January 20), and Dallas-Pittsburgh (March 22).

**4.8  B.  Larry Murphy and Ray Bourque**
Not one but two defensemen passed Tim Horton and took the lead among rearguards for most career games played in 1998–99. Murphy passed Horton on February 5, 1999, in his 1,447th league game; Bourque did it two months later on April 5, 1999.

## MOST GAMES PLAYED BY DEFENSEMEN[*]

| Player | Team | Seasons | GP |
|---|---|---|---|
| Larry Murphy | LA/Wash/Minn/ Pit/Tor/Det | 20 | 1,558 |
| Ray Bourque | Boston/Colorado | 21 | 1,532 |
| Tim Horton | Tor/NYR/Pit/Buf | 24 | 1,446 |
| Harry Howell | NYR/Cal/LA | 22 | 1,411 |
| Paul Coffey | Edm/Pit/LA/ Det/Htf/Phi/Car | 20 | 1,391 |
| Larry Robinson | Mtl/LA | 20 | 1,384 |

[*]*Current to 1999–2000*

**4.9  D.  Martin Brodeur**
To date, five netminders have scored seven times in NHL action, but none, until Martin Brodeur's goal on February 15, 2000, were game winners. Brodeur was credited with the goal after Philadelphia misplayed the puck into its own vacated net on a delayed penalty. The Devils' goalie was the last player to touch the puck. "If I'm going to score, it might as well be a game winner," said Brodeur after the 4–2 win. It was the second NHL

goal of his career. And there could have been another. Brodeur almost netted a goal late in the game. In the dying seconds he launched a high shot at the empty net, only to have the puck swatted out of the air by a Flyer.

**4.10  C.  Doug Harvey**
In 1961, Montreal traded six-time Norris Trophy-winner (top defenseman) Doug Harvey to the New York Rangers for tough guy Leapin' Lou Fontinato. The Canadiens, looking to toughen up their lineup, chose well: Fontinato led the league with 167 penalty minutes in 1961–62. But Harvey, who became the Rangers' player-coach, won the Norris a record seventh time.

**4.11  D.  More than 50 points back**
If Brian Leetch, Ray Bourque and Paul Coffey have anyone to thank for establishing today's rushing style of play for defensemen, it's Bobby Orr. During his dozen NHL years, Orr put the rush back into the blueliner's game, and the term superstar into the hockey lexicon for defensemen. His second scoring title in 1974–75 was his last great hurrah. He led the league in points and assists and broke his own rearguard record with 46 goals, 18 more than Canadiens defenseman Guy Lapointe's runner-up total of 28 goals. More impressive, Orr finished a staggering 59 points ahead of second-place D-man Denis Potvin of the New York Islanders. Potvin had 76 points to Orr's 135.

**4.12  B.  11 years**
At the time, no one in the hockey world could imagine another defenseman smashing Bobby Orr's 46-goal effort in 1974–75— or at least not in just 11 years. But in 1985–86, Paul Coffey pulled off what looked impossible and lit 48 red lights to break Orr's mark by two goals. It was an epic season for Coffey, who established a number of other offensive standards for blueliners. He broke Ray Bourque's 17-game point streak with a remarkable 28-game span that included 55 points, and tied Tom Bladon's

1977–78 mark of eight points in a game. Coffey played the last game of the season needing just two goals to hit the coveted 50-goal mark, and one point to tie Orr's record point total of 139. But the Norris Trophy winner went pointless, finishing with a head-turning 48 goals and 138 points.

### 4.13  A.  No wins

The 1974–75 Capitals established a number of spectacular NHL lows (some later broken by the hapless Ottawa Senators in the early 1990s). In fact, no team in league history has set more losing or winless streaks than Washington in their first year of play. It wasn't just bad, it was ugly. The Caps went 17 games without a win, 11 games without a victory at home, incurred 37 consecutive road losses and allowed an all-time record-high 446 goals. Their worst game was a 12–1 loss to Boston. To make sure the pain was real, the Caps recorded another 12–1 drubbing to Pittsburgh. They incurred five more losses in the double digits. The year was costly on the coaches, too. Three bench bosses were wasted, and 39 players made the rounds before the smoke cleared. Through it all, goalie Michel Belhumeur played 35 games and won none. He was responsible for 162 goals, or a monster 36 per cent of the season's goals-allowed count. His goals-against average was embarrassing, too—more than five goals per game. Belhumeur (which in French means good humour) must have had a *great* sense of humour to survive with his confidence intact. He played another seven games for Washington the following season and, again, like the previous year, did not win any of them. Belhumeur never played in the NHL again.

### 4.14  A.  Ron Grahame was traded by Boston for Ray Bourque

If you stick around long enough in hockey there is no telling who you'll cross paths with. In a game against Toronto on October 4, 1999, Bourque played in front of Boston rookie netminder John Grahame, the son of Ron Grahame. Ron Grahame signed as a free agent with the Bruins in 1977, then two years later was traded to Los Angeles for the Kings' first-round pick in 1979's NHL draft. Who did Boston choose with that pick? Ray Bourque.

**4.15  B.  48 inches**

In an effort to increase scoring in 1999–2000, the NHL implemented new restrictions governing catching gloves, which they downsized by two inches to 48 inches. Some goalies felt more susceptible to injury with less catching glove. "There's no margin for error anymore," Toronto's Curtis Joseph told the *National Post.* "If you close your hand too fast and catch a shot on the end of your glove, you're in trouble." The evidence backed up Joseph's claim. In a one-week stretch in December 1999, four goalies— Phoenix's Sean Burke, Chris Osgood of Detroit, Los Angeles' Stephane Fiset and Jocelyn Thibault of Chicago—were all out of action with hand injuries. With shots coming harder than ever, Joseph began putting his trapper only halfway on his hand and taping it in place.

**4.16  C.  Brian Leetch**

In 1998–99, three of the top shot-blockers played for the New York Rangers, but no player blocked more than Brian Leetch, with 212 shots blocked. Other top-flight defensive names— including Ray Bourque (113 shots blocked), Rob Blake (139) and Al MacInnis (128)—don't even approach the numbers of the Rangers' captain. It's both a science and an art. Timing is essential. "There are certain ways to go down," says Craig Ludwig, another premier shot-blocker (122 shots blocked). "If you are seven or eight feet from the guy, you do not go down on both knees and have your head in the way. You have to be smart enough to go down when your head is facing the corner and not the net, because they are trying to score a goal and you have to keep your head away from the play. But half the time you do not think about it. It just becomes part of your game," the veteran rearguard said in a *National Post* story.

## The NHL's Top Shot-Blockers of 1998–99

| Player | Team | GP | SB | Avg. |
|---|---|---|---|---|
| Brian Leetch | NYR | 82 | 212 | 2.58 |
| Ulf Samuelsson | NYR/Detroit | 71 | 179 | 2.52 |
| Peter Popovic | NYR | 68 | 178 | 2.61 |
| Igor Ulanov | Montreal | 76 | 163 | 2.14 |
| Ken Daneyko | New Jersey | 82 | 159 | 1.93 |
| Mattias Norstrom | Los Angeles | 78 | 157 | 2.01 |
| Mattias Ohlund | Vancouver | 74 | 154 | 2.08 |

**4.17  A.  Bobby Orr**

Pat Quinn played 617 NHL games, including playoffs. He scored 132 points and recorded 971 penalty minutes. As a brute defenseman with few skills, almost all of that nine-year career has been forgotten, except for one incident during his rookie playoff season. Quinn is long remembered for his bone-crushing body check on the great Bobby Orr. It happened at Boston Garden on April 2, 1969, as Orr was fighting off Toronto's Brit Selby for the puck. The Bruins defenseman lost control of the puck between his legs. Quinn motored in at full speed and pounded the pre-occupied Orr with such force that the two were thrown in opposite directions. Orr collapsed, knocked out cold near the boards. Quinn got a five-minute elbowing major and a rough time from Bruin fans, who tried to exact their own revenge on him. Quinn swung his stick to defend himself and broke a pane of protective glass, which showered down on a policeman. The fans were screaming "We want Quinn" as the besieged rookie escaped to the Toronto dressing room. Shaken, Orr stumbled off the ice to the Boston room. The Bruins annihilated Toronto 10-0 and swept the quarterfinal series.

#### 4.18  C.  Martin Brodeur

Aside from Martin Brodeur himself, perhaps no individual is more responsible for his sparkling goalie average than Jacques Lemaire, the coach who brought the trap style of play to the New Jersey Devils. With a crack defensive game plan that smothered opponents in the neutral zone, Lemaire gave the Devils a Stanley Cup championship and Brodeur a 2.19 goals-against average, the best during the 1990s.

---

## THE 1990's TOP GOALS-AGAINST AVERAGES[*]

| Player | Team | GAA |
|---|---|---|
| Martin Brodeur | New Jersey | 2.19 |
| Dominik Hasek | Chicago/Buffalo | 2.28 |
| Chris Osgood | Detroit | 2.33 |
| Ed Belfour | Chi/SJ/Dallas | 2.44 |
| Patrick Roy | Montreal/Colorado | 2.59 |
| Trevor Kidd | Cal/Car/Fla | 2.64 |

[*]*Based on a calendar decade*

---

#### 4.19  A.  Five shots

Turnbull established two records that night in February 1977. He was the first (and to date the only) rearguard to score five goals in a single NHL game and the only five-goal scorer in league history to score five times on just five shots—two against the Red Wings' Eddie Giacomin and three against backup Jim Rutherford.

#### 4.20  B.  Two sweater numbers

Chicago fans will long remember their famous No. 7, but when Chelios was dealt to Detroit in 1999 they not only had to endure their once-favourite rearguard in the much-hated Red Wing jersey, but the fact that he also sported an unfamiliar number on his back: No. 24. Chelios gave up his lucky digit because Detroit had retired No. 7 in honour of Ted Lindsay. Why did he choose No. 24 in Detroit? Because it was his playing number in Montreal before he was traded to the Blackhawks in 1990. Chelios made the switch to No. 7 in Chicago because longtime Hawk defenseman Doug Wilson was wearing No. 24 at the time.

**4.21  D.  Patrick Roy**
Roy had quite a week in late March 1999. In three home games he posted a 3–0–0 record and a wicked 1.67 goals-against average before being named NHL player of the week. The Colorado goalie defeated Vancouver 5–2, Washington 3–1 and Los Angeles 7–2. The March 28 victory over the Kings was especially gratifying. It was Roy's 506th career win, enabling him to surpass Jacques Plante for the most wins by a goalie in NHL history. To reach that plateau Roy won 407 regular-season games and 99 postseason matches.

# Game 4

# CAPTAINS OF TIME

Before Ray Bourque's trade to the Colorado Avalanche in March 2000, he was the longest-serving captain in NHL history. His 15-year captaincy in Boston surpassed Steve Yzerman's. Through 1999–2000, Yzerman wore the Red Wings' "C" for 14 seasons and more than 1,000 games. In this game, match the NHL captains in the left column with the teams they led.

(*Solutions are on page 120*)

| | | |
|---|---|---|
| 1. _____ Johnny Buyck | A. | Washington Capitals |
| 2. _____ George Armstrong | B. | Montreal Canadiens |
| 3. _____ Pierre Pilote | C. | Vancouver Canucks |
| 4. _____ Alex Delvecchio | D. | Toronto Maple Leafs |
| 5. _____ Jean Béliveau | E. | New York Rangers |
| 6. _____ Bob Gainey | F. | St. Louis Blues |
| 7. _____ Bill Cook | G. | Toronto Maple Leafs |
| 8. _____ Brian Sutter | H. | Montreal Canadiens |
| 9. _____ Hap Day | I. | Detroit Red Wings |
| 10. _____ Stan Smyl | J. | Chicago Blackhawks |
| 11. _____ Rod Langway | K. | Boston Bruins |

# 5
# TRUE OR FALSE?

True or False? NHLers can attend a special hockey school geared to improve their fighting skills. Neither Wayne Gretzky nor Gordie Howe ever scored on Ken Dryden. The so-called Czechmate Line of 1999–2000 was iced by the Pittsburgh Penguins. In this chapter, we shift from multiple-choice questions and give you a 50–50 chance on head crunchers like these.

*(Answers are on page 69)*

**5.1**  The Atlanta Thrashers' first NHL victory was against the New York Islanders, the same team that the original Atlanta team (the Flames) beat for its first win 27 years earlier. **True or False?**

**5.2**  As in the NFL, it is illegal to make a throat-slashing motion towards an opponent in the NHL. **True or False?**

**5.3**  No players converted to wearing face shields after Bryan Berard's terrible eye injury in March 2000. **True or False?**

**5.4**  Neither Wayne Gretzky nor Gordie Howe ever scored a goal against Ken Dryden. **True or False?**

**5.5**  Scotty Bowman was the first person to coach in five decades of NHL action. **True or False?**

**5.6**  Mario Lemieux was the youngest player to be inducted into the Hockey Hall of Fame. **True or False?**

**5.7** Although NHL All-Star games had been played since 1947, it wasn't until 1968 that a player wore a helmet at the annual event. **True or False?**

**5.8** Dave Keon is the only Toronto Maple Leaf player to win the Conn Smythe Trophy as playoff MVP. **True or False?**

**5.9** The Montreal Canadiens usually play the Calgary Flames on New Year's Eve. **True or False?**

**5.10** Following the Montreal Canadiens in 1981–82, the Detroit Red Wings became the second NHL club to record 2,000 league wins. **True or False?**

**5.11** No NHL All-Star game has ever been played penalty-free. **True or False?**

**5.12** Coach Pat Burns has won the Jack Adams Award as coach of the year with every NHL team he has coached to date. **True or False?**

**5.13** Defensive great Larry Robinson never scored a hat trick in his 20-year career. **True or False?**

**5.14** CBC's "Hockey Night in Canada" is North America's longest-running TV sports program. **True or False?**

**5.15** Bobby and Dennis Hull are the only brothers to each record five-goal games in the NHL. **True or False?**

**5.16** Wayne Gretzky scored more career goals on the road than at his home arena in regular-season play. **True or False?**

**5.17** The old Colorado Rockies had a different head coach in each of the club's six NHL seasons. **True or False?**

**5.18** The so-called Czechmate Line of 1999–2000 was iced by the Pittsburgh Penguins. **True or False?**

**5.19** Toronto tough guy Eddie Shack was the first player in All-Star history to be named game MVP. **True or False?**

**5.20** When Gordie Howe broke Maurice Richard's career record for All-Star points in 1963, Howe netted his winning point by assisting on a goal by Richard's younger brother, Henri. **True or False?**

**5.21** Wearing hard-cap elbow pads is considered illegal in the NHL. **True or False?**

**5.22** The Colorado Avalanche is the only team in NHL history to win the Stanley Cup in its first season in a new city. **True or False?**

**5.23** Wayne Gretzky was the first player traded among the core group of Oilers from Edmonton's dynasty team in the 1980s. **True or False?**

**5.24** Paul Coffey won the Norris Trophy (best defenseman) in 1983–84, the year he placed second to teammate Wayne Gretzky in the NHL scoring race. **True or False?**

**5.25** The NHL's new goal-scoring award, presented for the first time in 1998–99, honoured Maurice Richard, who led the league in goals more often than any other NHLer. **True or False?**

**5.26** A Canadian was the first winner of the Lester Patrick Trophy for outstanding hockey service in the United States. **True or False?**

**5.27** No father and son have both centred the same wingers. **True or False?**

**5.28** The first goalie to wear a mask regularly in the NHL was Jacques Plante in 1959–60. Interestingly, Plante donned his mask for the first time on Halloween, October 31, 1959. **True or False?**

**5.29** No two brothers have ever led the NHL in scoring. **True or False?**

**5.30** No player—rookie or otherwise—has scored more goals in a season since Teemu Selanne potted 76 in his rookie campaign of 1992–93. **True or False?**

**5.31** No former first-overall draft pick (who went on to become an NHL general manager) has ever drafted a first-overall pick in the Entry Draft. **True or False?**

**5.32** Mario Lemieux scored more points in the playoffs than in the regular season in 1990–91, the year he played only 26 regular-season games. **True or False?**

**5.33** After tough guy Bob Probert earned his 3,000th penalty minute in 1999–2000, he became the NHL's new penalty-minute leader. **True or False?**

**5.34** No player in NHL history has ever played his first game as team captain. **True or False?**

**5.35** Mario Lemieux is the first former pro athlete to acquire a controlling stake in a franchise he once played for. **True or False?**

**5.36** In his first game against Calgary after his 1999 trade to Colorado, sniper Theo Fleury failed to score against his former team. **True or False?**

**5.37** To improve their pugilistic skills, players can attend a hockey fight school. **True or False?**

**5.38** No goalie has ever recorded more shutouts than wins in a season. **True or False?**

**5.39** In 1999 there were no surviving members of Detroit's first Stanley Cup-winning team from 1936. **True or False?**

**5.40** The Washington Capitals presented Dale Hunter with a horse trailer as a retirement gift in March 2000. **True or False?**

# TRUE OR FALSE?
## Answers

**5.1**   True
Talk about a sense of history. First, the Thrashers invite Atlanta's first coach in 1972, Bernie Geoffrion, to drop the ceremonial first puck on October 2, 1999. Then, in another twist, the inaugural wins of both the Atlanta Flames and the Atlanta Thrashers turned out to be victories against the same team, the New York Islanders. The old Flames defeated the Isles 3–2 for their first win on October 7, 1972, and, 27 years later, the Thrashers captured their first victory by whitewashing New York 2–0 on October 14, 1999. It was the Thrashers' fourth NHL game and their first on the road. Let's hope the Flames and the Thrashers share nothing more than inaugural wins. Eight years after that first victory, the Flames moved to Calgary.

**5.2**   True
After the Florida Panthers' Peter Worrell made a throat-slashing motion three times towards the New Jersey Devils' bench in a game March 19, 2000, the NHL sent a memo to all teams stating that the league had joined the NFL in banning the gesture. The Devils' Scott Niedermayer had provoked the incident by chopping Worrell in the head with his stick. Niedermayer

received a 10-game suspension and had to forfeit U.S.$152,343.74 in salary.

**5.3    False**

Within days of seeing what happened to Bryan Berard, whose sight and career were threatened after a terrible eye injury, at least four NHLers—Mathieu Schneider, Theo Fleury, Radek Bonk and Jeff Halpern—donned visors. Six members of the New York Islanders added visors within a week, as did a few others, including Chicago's Bryan McCabe, Montreal's Shayne Corson and Tampa Bay's Vincent LeCavalier.

**5.4    True**

Neither Wayne Gretzky nor Gordie Howe ever scored on Ken Dryden, because neither of hockey's all-time leading scorers ever *played* against the great Canadiens netminder. Dryden's NHL career was bookended by Howe's first retirement in 1971 (before he joined the WHA) and his last NHL season, 1979–80; and Gretzky's first season, 1979–80. Dryden played his first six NHL games in 1970–71, never once facing Howe. When Dryden retired nine years later in 1978–79, both Howe and Gretzky were still in the WHA.

**5.5    True**

When Scotty Bowman stepped behind the Detroit bench on January 2, 2000, he became the first person in NHL history to coach in five decades. Bowman, who won more than 1,100 games during the 1960s, '70s, '80s, '90s and 2000, has coached eight Stanley Cup champions, an NHL record equalled only by Montreal legend Toe Blake. One more Cup for Bowman and he ties the Boston Celtics' Red Auerbach for most championships by a coach in the four major pro sports.

**5.6** **False**

Lemieux, at age 32, was one year older than 31-year-old Bobby Orr when each was inducted into the Hall of Fame. Both Orr and Lemieux had the Hall's mandatory three-year waiting periods waived and were honoured in the year they retired: Orr in 1979 and Lemieux in 1997. Orr is still the youngest person to enter the Hall of Fame.

**5.7** **True**

The first time a player wore head protection in an NHL All-Star game was in 1968, when Toronto's Brian Conacher donned a helmet. Conacher was prompted to don headgear by the tragic death of Bill Masterton, who had died from an on-ice injury just a day earlier. Prior to 1947 the NHL held three charity games involving All-Stars, including the inaugural benefit game to honour Ace Bailey. In that 1934 game, defenseman Eddie Shore of the Boston Bruins wore a helmet.

**5.8** **True**

Since the playoff MVP trophy was first presented in 1965, the Maple Leafs have reached the Cup finals only once, in 1967, when Keon was named playoff MVP. To date, no other Maple Leaf has won the trophy named in honour of Toronto legend Conn Smythe.

**5.9** **True**

Few events have stopped the annual New Year's Eve matchup between Calgary and Montreal. In 1999, it was the Y2K bug. Fearing long flight delays, the NHL scheduled only two league games and cancelled the traditional Canadiens-Flames December 31 contest. Calgary has a 1990s New Year's record of four wins and three losses against Montreal.

**5.10 False**

The Boston Bruins were the second NHL franchise to net their 2,000th NHL win. It came on November 2, 1989, in a 5–4 overtime victory over Los Angeles. The Red Wings celebrated win number 2,000 in 1996–97.

**5.11 False**

The NHL All-Star game has undergone many format changes. Recently, it has changed from a competitive game to a showcase event, eliminating much of the rough play common to earlier games. The 1992 All-Star game marked the first penalty-free game in history, as Campbell whipped Wales 10–6.

**5.12 True**

A great motivator with young teams, Burns has been named bench boss of the year with every club he has coached to date, including the three Original Six teams of Montreal (1989), Toronto (1993) and Boston (1998).

**5.13 False**

Twenty-year man Larry Robinson only scored one hat trick his entire NHL career. It came on December 19, 1985, in a 5–4 Canadiens loss to the Quebec Nordiques.

**5.14 True**

"Hockey Night in Canada" premiered on the CBC in 1952, establishing its credentials as North America's longest-running TV sports show.

**5.15 False**

The only brothers to notch five-goal games are Cy and Corb Denneny, who each recorded six-goal games in 1920–21. Neither Bobby nor Dennis Hull ever scored five goals in a game.

**5.16 False**

During his 20-year career Gretzky scored 492 goals at home and 401 goals on the road, not including a goal scored at a neutral-site game in 1993–94.

**5.17 True**

Colorado's first go-round in the NHL was an unmitigated disaster. The Rockies' six-year run from 1975 to 1982 included seven coaches. First, Johnny Wilson was replaced by Pat Kelly, who was then blown out in favour of Aldo Guidolin; who was later fired to hire Don Cherry; who was exchanged a year later for Billy MacMillan; who was dropped to bring in Bert Marshall; who lasted mere months before Marshall Johnston got the nod and finally the heave-ho as the last Rockies coach—their departures were tied to the team's dismal record. The Rockies failed to qualify for postseason play each and every year of their existence. The team won just 113 regular-season games in six seasons.

**5.18 False**

Although the 1999–2000 Penguins had seven regulars from the Czech Republic, the Czechmate Line was formed by the New York Rangers. In one 20-game stretch, wingers Jan Hlavac and Radek Dvorak, and centre Petr Nedved, scored 27 goals and 61 points.

**5.19 True**

He ran on his skates and generally acted like a buffoon, but Eddie "Clear the Track" Shack picked up the All-Star game's first MVP honour after scoring one goal in the 1962 event. The defending Stanley Cup champion, the Toronto Maple Leafs, defeated the NHL All-Stars 4–1.

**5.20 True**

At the 1963 All-Star game, Howe moved past Maurice Richard's All-Star career point total of nine, scoring his record-breaking

10th point by setting up a Henri Richard goal. Toronto tied the NHL All-Stars 3–3.

**5.21 True**

In an effort to soften elbow blows, the NHL deemed hard-cap elbow pads dangerous and illegal in 1999–2000. Although some players refused to give up the protection, the league viewed hard-covered caps as concussion causers. In response, manufacturers (including Jofa, whose pads are the choice of 85 per cent of NHLers) began phasing out production of the hard-cap pad in favour of softer caps covered with foam and synthetic leather. Jofa insisted that the new model was safer, and as protective, as the original.

**5.22 True**

After years of regular-season and playoff frustration, the Quebec Nordiques were sold to interests in Colorado; they won the Stanley Cup as the Avalanche in 1996. It was the first time an NHL team captured the Cup in its first year in a new city. The Avalanche celebrated with two championship parades: the official celebration in Denver and another for tortured Nordiques fans when they paraded the Cup through Quebec City.

**5.23 False**

Eight months before Gretzky was traded to Los Angeles in 1988, Edmonton general manager Glen Sather began the break-up of the Oilers dynasty by trading two-time Norris Trophy-winning defenseman Paul Coffey. Coffey, holding out to renegotiate his contract, was dealt to Pittsburgh in a seven-player swap on November 24, 1987. He was later followed by Gretzky, Messier, Kurri, Anderson and Fuhr.

**5.24 False**

The league's most prolific rearguard since Bobby Orr, Coffey finished second to Gretzky with 40 goals and 126 points in

1983–84, but failed to win top blueliner honours. Despite his stratospheric numbers, Coffey lost the Norris vote to Washington's Rod Langway, who had scored 93 points less. Langway netted just 33 points, but his steady play helped move the struggling Capitals out of the Patrick Division basement. The Washington rearguard also finished runner-up for the Hart Trophy as league MVP, an award almost never bestowed upon defensemen. Coffey finally won his first of three Norrises the following year; he was never a serious candidate for the Hart.

**5.25 False**

The NHL's new goal scorer's award is called the Maurice Richard Trophy, even though the Rocket led the league in goals only five times, one season less than Phil Esposito (six times) and two less than Bobby Hull (seven times). Three other NHLers are tied with Richard at five: Charlie Conacher, Gordie Howe and Wayne Gretzky.

**5.26 True**

The first winner of the NHL's Lester Patrick Trophy for service to hockey in America was Canadian-born Jack Adams in 1966. "Jolly" Jack turned the near-bankrupt Detroit Red Wings into a powerhouse during his 35-year tenure, producing a legacy of seven Stanley Cups between 1927–28 to 1961–62.

**5.27 True**

It has happened at least once. On November 11, 1964, Jimmy Peters Jr. was called up from the junior ranks for one game to centre Detroit's Gordie Howe, age 36, and Ted Lindsay, age 39. During the 1950s, Jimmy's dad, Jimmy Sr., also played on an interim basis between the two stars.

**5.28 False**

The story is part of hockey history; its conseqences changed the game forever. After receiving seven stitches to close a gash caused by an Andy Bathgate blast in a Rangers-Canadiens game, Plante returned wearing a crude fibreglass mask he had been trying out in practices. The date was November 1, one day after Halloween, 1959.

**5.29 False**
The only brothers to win the NHL scoring race are Doug and Max Bentley. During the 1940s, the scoring columns were rife with the Bentley name. On seven occasions, a Bentley led the league in either goals, assists or points, including three times when one of them won the scoring championship: Doug in 1942–43 and Max in 1945–46 and 1946–47.

**5.30 True**
To date, no one has topped Alexander Mogilny and Teemu Selanne's 76-goal outbursts of 1992–93. Mario Lemieux, who twice hit 69 goals in 1992–93 and 1995–96, has the next-highest goal counts (to date) since 1992–93.

**5.31 True**
Only two first-overall picks have ever become NHL general managers: Rejean Houle and Bobby Smith. Houle, general manager in Montreal, may have come the closest to realizing this rare feat during the 1999–2000 season. Struck by a parade of injuries, the Canadiens could have finished dead last, creating the opportunity for Houle, the first-overall pick in 1969, to make the first pick in the 2000 draft year—if he lasted that long in his job. But Montreal finished 18th overall.

**5.32 False**
page is
1 line
long
Chronic back problems limited Mario Lemieux to only 26 games and 45 points in 1990–91, but the Penguins sniper roared back in the postseason, scoring a personal best of 44 playoff points (in 23 games) to lead Pittsburgh to its first Stanley Cup. Lemieux tallied just one point more in regular-season action than in the playoffs.

**5.33 False**

In fact, Probert, thanks to his 3,000th penalty minute, now ranks sixth on the NHL's all-time list of penalty leaders, behind Dave Williams (3,966 minutes), Dale Hunter (3,565), Marty McSorley (3,381), Tim Hunter (3,146) and Chris Nilan (3,043).

**5.34 False**

It's not unusual for players to play their first NHL game as captain, but most of the time it happens with new franchises. The New York Rangers (Bill Cook), Chicago Blackhawks (Dick Irvin) and Detroit Red Wings (Art Duncan) were all captained by first-year NHL players. More recently, the Winnipeg Jets (Lars-Erik Sjoberg) and Edmonton Oilers (Ron Chipperfield) each entered the NHL with rookie captains, in 1979–80.

**5.35 True**

It was the second time Mario Lemieux saved the Pittsburgh Penguins. After reviving hockey's worst team in 1984–85, winning two Stanley Cups in the 1990s and retiring after claiming his sixth scoring championship in 1996–97, Lemieux returned to hockey in 1999 as the first player-turned-owner in major pro sports. His efforts saved the bankrupt Penguins from moving (probably to Portland). To do it, Lemieux raised U.S.$50 million in cash to operate the team and pay some debts. He received a $5-million payment from former co-owner Roger Marino and a $20-million ownership stake in the team (which was converted from the $32.5 million owed to him in deferment payments as a player).

**5.36 False**

Fleury averaged better than a point a game in 791 games with Calgary (830 points) but held nothing back in his first contest against his former team. He scored a goal and an assist in the 3–3 Colorado-Calgary match on March 30, 1999.

**5.37 True**

In the summer of 1999, Dustin McArthur, an Eastern Hockey League player, opened up the first hockey fight school in Sarnia, Ontario. McArthur's logic was simple. "By no means is it to create fighters," he said in a *National Post* story. "The idea is to teach hockey players how to best defend themselves." In the school's inaugural season, 30 students learned the fundamentals of boxing and hockey fighting, including how to punch, how to hold, how to tie up an opponent and how to duck.

**5.38 False**

It may be the only time in NHL history that a goalie recorded more shutouts than wins in one season. In 1928–29, league rules forbade forward passing in the attacking zone. Goalies such as George Hainsworth racked up record shutout totals that remain unchallenged today. In the nets for the lowly Pittsburgh Pirates was Joe Miller, who recorded only nine wins but registered 11 shutouts in the 44-game schedule. Miller won six of those shutouts and played to scoreless ties in the remaining five.

**5.39 False**

The Red Wings won the 1936 Stanley Cup—the first in franchise history—on a goal by Pete Kelly (in 1999, Kelly was the longest surviving member of the championship team). In the best-of-five finals against Toronto, Kelly scored the Cup winner in Game 4, defeating the Maple Leafs 3–2. "I wasn't even supposed to be on the ice," said Kelly in *Where Are They Now?* "I noticed Larry Aurie, one of our big guns, was tired and heading to the bench. I knew the coach wouldn't put me on, so I just jumped over the boards and ended up scoring the winning goal." Kelly's Cup-winner was his first of just three playoff goals. He also played for two defunct NHL teams, the St. Louis Eagles and the New York-Brooklyn Americans.

**5.40 True**

In a March 2000 ceremony, the Washington Capitals retired former captain Dale Hunter's No. 32, then presented him with a horse trailer (for his Ontario farm) and the actual penalty box from the USAir Arena. In attendance was Marcel Aubut, former owner of the Quebec Nordiques, the team with which Hunter spent his first seven NHL seasons.

# Game 5

# THE PUCK PUZZLE

In this game each word is connected in the same way as a regular crossword. Starting at square number one, work clockwise around the four concentric rings or towards the centre along the spokes, filling in the correct answer from the clues below. Each answer begins with the letter of the previous word. Determine word length by using the clue numbers (e.g., the answer to "Around, number one" is eight letters long, since the next clue is number three.)

*(Solutions are on page 121)*

### Around

1. 1960s Montreal enforcer, John _____

3. Digit on back of jersey

5. 1970 Red Wing, Mickey _____

7. Enhancing drug

9. _____ Lindros

10. Wendel _____

12. 1970s Buffalo/LA D-man, Jerry _____

14. 1970s Flyers sniper, Bill _____

16. Buffalo coach, Lindy _____

17. Club; NHL _____

18. Too many _____ on the ice

19. _____ Broten

20. 1970s Detroit winger, Nick _____

21. 1970s Ranger, Walt _____

22. 1980s Toronto-New Jersey winger, Jim _____

23. ID on back of sweater

24. 1990s Montreal-Anaheim tough guy, Todd _____

25. 1970s Flyer winger, Simon _____

26. Drive or _____ into the boards

27. 1980s journeyman winger with the Sabres, Pens, Devils, Gary _____

28. 2000 Dallas veteran, Kirk _____

29. 1990s Boston-Dallas winger, David _____

30. Scoring champ, Marcel _____

80

31. Old-timer Hab, _____ Lach
32. 1970s Boston's Derek _____
33. "Hockey _____ in Canada"
34. The Dallas Stars' state

**Towards Centre**

1. _____ "the Fog" Shero

2. The Blues' hometown
4. The goalie is _____ the pipes
6. _____ it up in the corners
8. Eight-time hab Cup-winner, Claude _____
11. Mario _____
13. New York team
15. Commissioner Gary _____

# 6
# TOWERS OF POWER

One of the game's biggest boosters of video tape is Paul Kariya. The Mighty Duck sniper analyzes stacks of tapes, studying players such as Jaromir Jagr. "When he came into the league I thought he was the best one-on-one player in the NHL," Kariya told the *National Post*. "But I think what he's developed over the past couple of years, is that he's learned to use his teammates well. I think he learned that from Mario Lemieux. Now you see Jaromir fading, making nice saucer passes through the middle, hitting the late man."

(*Answers are on page 87*)

**6.1** **Which sniper recorded the greatest margin in goals over the next top scorer—in one season?**
A. Bobby Hull
B. Wayne Gretzky
C. Brett Hull
D. Mario Lemieux

**6.2** **Who scored the most game-winning goals in his career?**
A. Guy Lafleur
B. Wayne Gretzky
C. Mike Bossy
D. Phil Esposito

**6.3** **Which rookie has recorded the most points in a season since Teemu Selanne's mind-numbing 132-point year in 1992–93?**
A. Joe Juneau
B. Mikael Renberg
C. Eric Lindros
D. Jason Allison

**6.4**  As of 1999–2000, how many career hat tricks did Jaromir Jagr have among his 387 goals?
A.  Six career hat tricks
B.  Nine career hat tricks
C.  12 career hat tricks
D.  13 career hat tricks

**6.5**  Which brother combination has scored the most goals in one NHL season?
A.  Maurice and Henri Richard
B.  Bobby and Dennis Hull
C.  Pavel and Valeri Bure
D.  Wayne and Brent Gretzky

**6.6**  How many different NHL players won scoring titles during the 1990s?
A.  Two players
B.  Three players
C.  Four players
D.  Five players

**6.7**  How many NHLers are known to have broken 100 M.P.H. in slap shot competition?
A.  About 10 players
B.  About 20 players
C.  About 30 players
D.  About 40 players

**6.8**  What is the longest time Montreal Canadiens superstar Guy Lafleur went without scoring a goal during his 17-year career?
A.  Four periods
B.  Four games
C.  Four weeks
D.  Four years

**6.9** Wayne Gretzky holds the mark for winning an NHL scoring race by the largest margin. What was Gretzky's record-setting lead?

A. 19 points
B. 39 points
C. 59 points
D. 79 points

**6.10** Which NHL player reached the 50-goal plateau for the first time in his career in a game played at a non-NHL arena?

A. Theo Fleury
B. Brendan Shanahan
C. Pavel Bure
D. Pierre Turgeon

**6.11** In Wayne Gretzky's record 92-goal season, 1981–82, how many games did the Great One go goal-less in the 80-game schedule?

A. None
B. Between one and 10 games
C. Between 11 and 20 games
D. More that 20 games

**6.12** In his record-setting 215-point season, how many games did Wayne Gretzky go without a point in the 80-game schedule?

A. None
B. Three games
C. Six games
D. Nine games

**6.13** Which player won the NHL scoring race playing the lowest percentage of games in a season? (For example, if a player won the scoring race playing 70 games of an 82-game schedule, his percentage would be 85 per cent.)

    A. Bobby Orr

    B. Wayne Gretzky

    C. Mario Lemieux

    D. Jaromir Jagr

**6.14** How many NHL games did it take Brett Hull to score 610 goals, the career goal count his father Bobby Hull amassed in 1,063 NHL games?

    A. 837 games

    B. 937 games

    C. 1,037 games

    D. 1,137 games

**6.15** Which veteran NHL superstar did not play in any of the five Canada Cup series held between 1976 and 1991?

    A. Steve Yzerman

    B. Dominik Hasek

    C. Brian Leetch

    D. Brett Hull

**6.16** According to Brett Hull, from where on the ice does he score at least half his goals?

    A. The point

    B. The slot

    C. The face-off circles

    D. In the crease

**6.17** Detroit's 1999–2000 foward line of Brendan Shanahan, Steve Yzerman and Pat Verbeek boasted three of the NHL's best snipers. As of 1999–2000, how many *career* goals had the trio scored?

A. Less than 1,000 career goals

B. Between 1,000 and 1,500 career goals

C. Between 1,500 and 2,000 career goals

D. More than 2,000 career goals

**6.18** How often has an NHL scoring leader recorded more than 100 penalty minutes in the same year he won the Art Ross Trophy?

A. It has never happened

B. Only once

C. Five times

D. 10 times

**6.19** Which NHLer holds the distinction of scoring the most points in a season while collecting fewer than 10 minutes in penalties?

A. Paul Kariya

B. Wayne Gretzky

C. Mike Bossy

D. Johnny Bucyk

**6.20** What is the closest in penalty minutes an NHL scoring leader has come to leading the league in box time that same season?

A. Within five minutes

B. Between 10 and 20 minutes

C. Between 20 and 40 minutes

D. On one occasion a scoring leader led the league in penalty minutes

**6.21** What is the fewest number of NHL career goals scored by a
player *after* he recorded a 50-goal season?
A. Less than 10 goals
B. Between 10 and 30 goals
C. Between 30 and 50 goals
D. More than 50 goals

**6.22** Who was the only sniper to record four consecutive 50-goal
seasons in the 1990s?
A. Pat LaFontaine
B. Jaromir Jagr
C. John LeClair
D. Brett Hull

# TOWERS OF POWER
## Answers

**6.1**   C.  Brett Hull
In 1990–91, Hull banged home a career-high 86 goals, finishing
35 goals ahead of runners-up Steve Yzerman (51) and Theo
Fleury (51). Hull's 35-goal margin is the largest spread for a goal
leader in NHL history; his 86-goal total is the NHL's third-highest
goal count ever.

**6.2**   D.  Phil Esposito
In his era no one was better at scoring from the slot than Phil
Esposito. He endured his share of whacks, cross-checks and
elbows, but wouldn't be moved or outmuscled from his favourite
position in front of the net. Among his career total of 717 goals,
Espo scored 100 game winners, the most among all NHLers. Guy
Lafleur recorded 97 game-winning goals; Wayne Gretzky, 91;
Mike Gartner, 90; Glenn Anderson, 85; and Mike Bossy, 82.
Esposito's actual numbers may be higher considering statistics in

this category only date to 1967–68, four seasons after Espo began his career in 1963–64.

**6.3 B. Mikael Renberg**
Mikael Renberg was one of the first Flyers to benefit offensively from the play of Eric Lindros. In his rookie season in Philadelphia, the Swedish winger scored 82 points, currently the highest point total by an NHL freshman since Teemu Selanne netted 132 in 1992–93. Renberg finished first among rookies in goals (38), points (82) and shots (195) in 1993–94. He also broke Jorgen Pettersson's NHL record of 37 goals by a Swedish rookie (1980-81).

**6.4 A. Six career hat tricks**
In the 10 years since joining the NHL in 1990, Jagr, a four-time league scoring champion, has managed only six regular-season hat tricks and just one playoff hat trick. His best year was 1999–2000, when he increased his career count of four hat tricks by 50 per cent. According to the scoring champ, that's just his style. "I'm just that kind of guy. If I score a goal and we get the lead, I don't go for more. I just like to have fun," Jagr admitted to hockey writer Dave Morinari.

**6.5 C. Pavel and Valeri Bure**
Bobby and Dennis Hull's NHL-record 88-goal count in 1968–69 was safe for 31 years, until the Bures combined for 93 goals in 1999–2000. It was Pavel's 54th of the season that broke the record to give the brothers a combined 89 goals, one more than the Hulls' long-surviving total. "We sat down and counted," Valeri said to the *Hockey News*. "We said, 'OK, there's 20 games left between the two of us and we have to score five goals.' We figured we could do it." By the year's end, Pavel had scored a league-leading 58 with Florida, while younger brother Valeri notched 35 for the Flames.

## TOP-SCORING BROTHER COMBINATIONS*

| Brothers | Team | Year | Goals | Combined Total |
|---|---|---|---|---|
| Pavel Bure | Florida | 1999-00 | 58 | 93 |
| Valeri Bure | Calgary | 1999-00 | 35 | |
| | | | | |
| Bobby Hull | Chicago | 1968-69 | 58 | 88 |
| Dennis Hull | Chicago | 1968-69 | 30 | |
| | | | | |
| Bobby Hull | Chicago | 1970-71 | 44 | 84 |
| Dennis Hull | Chicago | 1970-71 | 40 | |
| | | | | |
| Peter Stastny | Quebec | 1982-83 | 47 | 83 |
| Marian Stastny | Quebec | 1982-83 | 36 | |
| | | | | |
| Pierre Turgeon | NYI | 1992-93 | 58 | 83 |
| Sylvain Turgeon | Ottawa | 1992-93 | 25 | |
| | | | | |
| Peter Stastny | Quebec | 1981-82 | 46 | 81 |
| Marian Stastny | Quebec | 1981-82 | 35 | |
| | | | | |
| Bobby Hull | Chicago | 1971-72 | 50 | 80 |
| Dennis Hull | Chicago | 1971-72 | 30 | |
| | | | | |
| Joe Mullen | Calgary | 1988-89 | 51 | 80 |
| Brian Mullen | NYR | 1988-89 | 29 | |

*Current to 1999–2000

## 6.6   B.   Three players

Talk about domination. Wayne Gretzky, Mario Lemieux and Jaromir Jagr were the only NHLers to capture scoring titles during the 1990s. In fact, you have to go all the way back to 1979–80 to find another name at the top of the scoring chart: Marcel Dionne of the Los Angeles Kings. In that 20-year stretch, Gretzky won 10 titles; Lemieux, six; and Jagr, four.

**6.7    A.  About 10 players**

In hardest-shot events at the NHL All-Star game, only a few players have ever fired a puck at 100 m.p.h. In 1999-2000, just five players qualified: Glen Murray of Los Angeles (103.5 m.p.h.), Fredrik Modin of Tampa Bay (102.0 m.p.h.), Rob Blake of the Kings (100.7 m.p.h.), Chris Therien of Philadelphia (100.6 m.p.h.), Bryan Muir of Chicago (100.4 m.p.h.) and Sheldon Souray of New Jersey (100.0 m.p.h.). In previous years only four other NHL skaters are known to have hit 100 m.p.h., including Dave Manson (100.8 m.p.h.), Tomas Sandstrom (100.7 m.p.h.), Al MacInnis (100.4 m.p.h.) and master blaster Al Iafrate, who holds the NHL record after discharging a 105.2 m.p.h. lightning bolt at the 1993 All-Star game in Montreal. Shawn Heins of San Jose's American League team in Kentucky recorded two blasts of 105.5 m.p.h. and 106.1 m.p.h. in 1998–99; during the late 1960s, the great Bobby Hull reportedly fired slap shots clocked at 118.3 m.p.h.

**6.8    D.  Four years**

At his peak, NHL scoring leader Guy Lafleur seldom missed the net. He racked up six straight 50-goal seasons and led Montreal to six Stanley Cups during the 1970s. But when he scored his 518th goal on October 25, 1984, it would be his last for four years—until he ended his premature retirement and returned to the league as a New York Ranger in 1988. Lafleur's next NHL marker, number 519, came on October 16, 1988, a four-year wait between red lights. (Ironically, Lafleur's 519th was assisted on by Marcel Dionne. Seventeen years earlier, Lafleur and Dionne went first and second overall in the 1971 NHL draft.) The Flower's comeback lasted three seasons, as chants of "Guy, Guy, Guy" once again filled arenas throughout the league.

**6.9    D.  79 points**
In 1983–84, Gretzky tallied 205 points for the Edmonton Oilers, 79 more than runner-up Paul Coffey. Winning the scoring race by such a wide gap was routine for Gretzky in his prime; five times he led his closest pursuer by more than 70 points. In fact, during a six-year span from 1981–82 to 1986–87, the Great One's average margin of victory over the second-place finisher was an astounding 73 points. His off-the-radar numbers were due to his remarkable assist totals, which, in some seasons, totalled more than the points amassed by his nearest competitor.

**6.10   C.  Pavel Bure**
The Russian Rocket reached the 50-goal plateau for the first time in his career on March 1, 1993, scoring on goalie Grant Fuhr during a Canucks-Sabres game at Hamilton's Copps Coliseum. The match was one of several neutral-site encounters staged in the NHL that season. Bure is the only player to hit the 50-goal milestone for the first time at a non-NHL rink.

**6.11   D.  More than 20 games**
No season in NHL history can compare to 1981–82, the year of the Wayne Gretzky show. To amass hockey's highest goal total of 92, Gretzky set some of the league's greatest standards, including his 50-goals-in-39-games mark, which came before the New Year and in 11 fewer games than anyone else had done before. Impressive, but Gretzky also scored a whopping 15 goals on just 32 shots in a five-game highlight reel. Then he demolished Phil Esposito's 76-goal record in just 64 games (Espo needed 78 games). Gretzky's season included seven hat tricks, two four-goal games and a milestone five-goal match. He scored 42 goals in the final 41 Oiler games. His worst run was a six-game drought in mid-March. In all, Gretzky didn't score in 25 of 80 Edmonton games, but still potted 92.

**6.12  B.  Three games**
During his monumental 215-point season in 1985–86, Gretzky failed to score a point in three games: his 10th game against Buffalo, his 50th versus Chicago and his 69th, again, against the Sabres. Before he got to 215, Gretzky had three-point nights 40 times and 21 four-pointers. His best night was December 11, when he notched a record-tying seven assists in the highest-scoring game in NHL history, a 12–9 Oilers win over Chicago. Gretzky's assist total of 163 proved to be better than any other player's point total. (Mario Lemieux had 141 points to finish a distant second to Gretzky's 215.) It was the Great One's fourth and final 200-point season.

**6.13  C.  Mario Lemieux**
It might be the greatest comeback in hockey. During his 1992–93 bid to eclipse Wayne Gretzky's record 215-point total, Lemieux was diagnosed with Hodgkin's disease after doctors found a cancerous lymph node in his neck. Lemieux's recovery amazed even his doctors. After two months of midseason radiation therapy Lemieux was back playing hockey. During the last 20 games he scored 59 points, demolishing a 12-point lead by Pat LaFontaine to win the title with 160 points, 12 more than LaFontaine. Lemieux won the scoring title playing the lowest percentage of games ever, just 60 of 84 games, or 71 per cent. In 1999–2000, Pittsburgh's Jaromir Jagr chalked up the next-lowest percentage, 77 per cent, seeing action in 63 of 82 games while capturing his fourth scoring crown.

**6.14  B.  937 games**
While comparisons are fun to make, they are difficult to judge. But let's do it anyway. Brett Hull reached 610 goals in three fewer seasons and 126 fewer games than his father, Bobby Hull. Beyond the goals, the two Hulls have achieved a number of significant milestones in their careers. Both Bobby and Brett have won the Hart Trophy as league MVP (Bobby twice and Brett

once); each have been named multiple times to All-Star teams (Bobby 12 times and Brett three times); each led the league in scoring (Bobby in seven seasons and Brett in three seasons); and, up until 1999, each had captured one Stanley Cup. Brett admits it's tough living up to the tag "Bobby Hull's son," but he now has his own place in history. Who's better? "No question, he's better," Brett said in a *Montreal Gazette* story. "I look at how he changed the game and how he shot the puck. To be part of that is an honour. I'm glad I'm his son."

**6.15 A. Steve Yzerman**
The five Canada Cups—1976, 1981, 1984, 1987 and 1991 —gave hockey fans a chance to see their favourite NHL players represent their countries in world competition. Inevitably, the overabundance of talent led to a number of NHL stars with impeccable credentials being cut, including Patrick Roy, Cam Neely and, perhaps the most perplexing cut of all, Steve Yzerman. In fact, Yzerman is probably the best player to be twice snubbed, first in 1987 and then in 1991. It was former coach Mike Keenan who, in 1991, yanked Yzerman, a player coming off a 51-goal season. The move was as unpopular as Marc Crawford's decision to overlook Mark Messier in favour of Rob Zamuner at the 1998 Olympics.

**6.16 B. The slot**
When Brett Hull scored his 600th career goal on December 31, 1999, he did it in his 900th game—third-fastest in the NHL behind Wayne Gretzky (718th game) and Mario Lemeiux (719th game). Hull achieved the feat on a typical play, a shot from the slot, while Dallas had the man advantage. "I think I've scored maybe half my goals from that spot," said Hull, who became just the 12th NHLer to net 600 goals. Hull and his father, Bobby, are the first father-son duo in the 600-goal club.

**6.17 C. Between 1,500 and 2,000 career goals**

During the 1999–2000 season, Dallas Stars coach Ken Hitchcock started using his top three forwards—Brett Hull, Mike Modano and Joe Nieuwendyk—on the same line. Although the high-flying trio totalled a combined 1,337 career goals, it couldn't match the staggering number scored by the Shanahan-Yzerman-Verbeek line in Detroit. The Red Wings unit had a combined 1,566 career goals: 627 by Yzerman, 500 by Verbeek and 439 by Shanahan. Shanahan, at age 30, found himself the junior to Yzerman, age 34, and Verbeek, age 36. "I have to get them water and stuff," Shanahan joked. "I hang up their equipment. Call me kid." The threesome took off after Detroit coach Scotty Bowman moved Verbeek to fill the spot vacated by injured Darren McCarty.

**6.18 D. 10 times**

In 82 NHL seasons the league's scoring leaders amassed 100 minutes in box time just 10 times. Chicago's Stan Mikita leads the pack with a 1–2 ranking, his highest totals peaking in 1964–65,

## MOST PENALTY MINUTES BY AN NHL SCORING LEADER*

| Player | Team | Year | Points | PIM |
|---|---|---|---|---|
| 1. Stan Mikita | Chicago | 1964-65 | 87 | 154 |
| 2. Stan Mikita | Chicago | 1963-64 | 89 | 146 |
| 3. Jean Béliveau | Montreal | 1955-56 | 88 | 143 |
| 4. Ted Lindsay | Detroit | 1949-50 | 78 | 141 |
| 5. Bobby Orr | Boston | 1969-70 | 120 | 125 |
| 6. Nels Stewart | Maroons | 1925-26 | 42 | 119 |
| 7. Gordie Howe | Detroit | 1953-54 | 81 | 109 |
| 8. Bobby Orr | Boston | 1974-75 | 135 | 101 |
| 9. Gordie Howe | Detroit | 1962-63 | 86 | 100 |
| 10. Mario Lemieux | Pittsburgh | 1988-89 | 199 | 100 |

*Current to 1999–2000*

when he sat out 154 minutes. In a five-year period Mikita won the Art Ross Trophy four times. Although his first two scoring championships were marred by 100-plus penalty-minute seasons, his final pair, in 1966–67 and 1967–68, featured uncharacteristic totals of just 12 and 14 minutes each, among the lowest ever by a scoring leader. "I thought I'd try to beat the other guy with my skills instead of knocking his head off," Mikita said.

**6.19 C. Mike Bossy**
As of 1999–2000, only three NHLers have combined a 100-point season with fewer than 10 minutes in penalties: Jean Ratelle, Mike Bossy and Johnny Bucyk. Of the three, Bossy had the most points. The New York Islanders sniper compiled 118 points while serving a mere eight minutes in penalties in 1983–84. Ratelle had 109 points and four minutes in box time in 1971–72; Bucyk sat out eight minutes during his 116-point season in 1970–71.

**6.20 A. Within five minutes**
No scoring leader has ever led the league in penalties during the same season, but in 1925-26 the Montreal Maroons' rookie sensation Nels Stewart came within one two-minute penalty of tying tough guy Bert Corbeau's league-high 121-minute mark. Stewart, who ruled the NHL with his 42-point rookie season, finished runner-up in box-time with 119 penalty minutes. A few other scoring leaders also came close in cooler time. Detroit's Ted Lindsay won the scoring crown and finished second in penalties with 141 minutes, just three minutes behind league leader Bill Ezinicki (144). In 1962–63, Stan Mikita won the Art Ross and accumulated 146 minutes—five behind the NHL leader, Vic Hadfield, who had 151.

**6.21 A. Less than 10 goals**
After scoring 50 goals in 49 games in 1993–94, Cam Neely managed only 53 goals over his last two seasons; Mike Bossy

scored just 38 more times after 1985–86's 68-goal effort; and Mickey Redmond potted 26 goals after his 51-goal year in 1973–74. All three 50-goal men suffered injuries that curtailed their goal production dramatically, but that was not the case for Bobby Hull. Hull leads all 50-goal scorers with just six NHL goals. After his fifth 50-goal season in 1971–72, he joined the renegade WHA and only returned to the NHL in 1979–80, scoring six times with the Hartford Whalers before finally retiring.

**6.22 D. Brett Hull**
John LeClair was poised to net his fourth straight 50-goal season in 1998–99, but in the first year of the Maurice Richard Trophy (top goal scorer), surprisingly, no NHLer (including LeClair) hit 50 goals. That left Hull as the only sniper with four consecutive 50-goal years during the 1990s. In fact, Hull did it five straight times between 1989–90 and 1993–94.

# Game 6

# UNUSUAL ENDINGS

When Gordie Howe hung up his blades in 1980, it wasn't as a Detroit Red Wing—the team he set the NHL record with for most seasons played. No, Howe's 25-year career with the Red Wings ended in 1971, years before he finally retired from NHL play. So with which NHL franchise did Gordie play his last season? Below are other hockey greats who finished their careers with clubs they weren't widely associated with. Match the team with the player.

*(Solutions are on page 121)*

**Part 1**

1. _____ Detroit's Gordie Howe
2. _____ Montreal's Larry Robinson
3. _____ Montreal's Jacques Plante
4. _____ Toronto's Darryl Sittler
5. _____ Chicago's Pierre Pilote
6. _____ Edmonton's Steve Smith
7. _____ Montreal's Doug Harvey
8. _____ Boston's Bobby Orr

A. Los Angeles Kings
B. Chicago Blackhawks
C. Calgary Flames
D. Hartford Whalers
E. St. Louis Blues
F. Boston Bruins
G. Detroit Red Wings
H. Toronto Maple Leafs

**Part 2**

1. _____ Montreal's Guy Lafleur
2. _____ Toronto's Borje Salming
3. _____ Chicago's Bobby Hull
4. _____ Washington's Dale Hunter
5. _____ Toronto's Andy Bathgate
6. _____ Quebec's Peter Stastny
7. _____ Buffalo's Rick Martin
8. _____ Chicago's Denis Savard

A. Hartford Whalers
B. Colorado Avalanche
C. Pittsburgh Penguins
D. St. Louis Blues
E. Quebec Nordiques
F. Detroit Red Wings
G. Tampa Bay Lightning
H. Los Angeles Kings

# 7

# READER REBOUND

Recognizing that our readers have as many—or more—great trivia questions as our research staff, we asked you (in previous trivia books) to send in your own hockey puzzlers. We received hundreds of letters with terrific queries from hockey fans from all over North America, some of which we've answered in this year's book. Congratulations! And thanks to all those who participated.

*(Answers are on page 101)*

**7.1** What was the name of the first NHL team to play in Philadelphia?

*Patrick Lavigne*
*Mont Tremblant, Quebec*

**7.2** Who was the NHL's last player-coach?

*Jimmy Sullivan*
*Freeport, New York*

**7.3** Edmonton Oiler forward Alexander Selivanov is married to the daughter of which NHL 500-goal scorer?

*Sonia Pannu*
*Victoria, British Columbia*

**7.4** What is the greatest number of Original Six teams one person has coached?

*Paul Shair*
*Toronto, Ontario*

**7.5** Which player delivered the most hits in 1999–2000?

*Robert Valenzano*
*Oak Lawn, Illinois*

**7.6** Who gave Pavel Bure his nickname—the Russian Rocket?

*Brandon Bieber*
*Humboldt, Saskatchewan*

**7.7** Who was smallest NHL player in 1999–2000?

*Ricky Watson*
*Niagara-on-the-Lake, Ontario*

**7.8** Who scored the first hat trick in the Atlanta Thrashers' history?

*Darren Cairns*
*Pleasant Grove, PEI*

**7.9** Why do the Montreal Canadiens always have good goaltenders?

*Andrew Casey*
*Montreal, Quebec*

**7.10** Who leads the NHL in career-overtime goals in the playoffs?

*Brian Cormier*
*St. Antoine de Kent, New Brunswick*

**7.11** Which NHL defenseman has won the most Norris Trophies as top blueliner?

*Jake Quaid*
*Lake Forest, Illinois*

**7.12** Who scored the last goal at McNichols Sports Arena and the first at the Pepsi Center in Colorado?

*Todd Vallee*
*Kitchener, Ontario*

**7.13** Who was the NHL's first Hispanic player?

*Jesse Nortman*
*Woodbury, New York*

**7.14** Which player won Stanley Cups on three different teams during the 1990s?

*Chris Reid*
*Gloucester, Ontario*

**7.15** Who was the first player to break Guy Lafleur's 28-game consecutive point-scoring streak, set in 1976–77?

*Timmy Iazzolino*
*Stoney Creek, Ontario*

**7.16** How many French-Canadian players played on the Montreal Canadiens in 1999–2000?

*Sammy Lazarus*
*Ottawa, Ontario*

**7.17** Who was the only NHLer to win the Hobey Baker as the top U.S. collegiate player and the Calder Trophy as NHL rookie of the year?

*Tammy Wright*
*Kensington, Connecticut*

**7.18** What do baseball great Hank Aaron and hockey broadcaster Don Cherry have in common?

*Steve Arbon*
*London, Ontario*

**7.19** Who was the first NHLer to score the first goal of the new millennium?

*Scott Ramsay*
*Abbotsford, British Columbia*

**7.20** Has Patrick Roy ever scored an empty-net goal?

Colin Schell
Fort St. John, British Columbia

# READER REBOUND
## Answers

**7.1** Long before the Flyers began hockey operations in 1967, another team wore the orange and black of Philadelphia. **The Philadelphia Quakers** joined the NHL in 1930–31, but, unlike the successful Flyers, failed to generate either hometown interest, goals or wins. Philly's first NHL team died a quick death, playing just one season (4–36–4) with a win percentage of .136, the worst in NHL history until the Washington Capitals' inaugural season of 1974–75.

**7.2** Centre **Charlie Burns** of the Minnesota North Stars was the last player-coach in the NHL. Better known as one of only four players to wear a helmet full-time in 1969–70, Burns was appointed Minnesota's bench boss in December when ill health forced Wren Blair to quit his coaching duties. Burns's double role may have split his effectiveness in both positions. He scored a career-low 16 points and led his North Stars to third place with a 19–35–22 record in the weak West Division.

**7.3** They say it was love at first sight when **Phil Esposito's** daughter, Carrie, met Russian winger Alexander Selivanov. Carrie was director of team services with Tampa Bay when Espo was the general manager of the team. "Alex came to me and asked if he could marry Carrie, before he asked her," Esposito confirmed in the *National Post*. "I said, 'You want to do what?' I thought he was just going to ask me for ice time!"

**7.4**    Although many coaches have bench-bossed multiple NHL teams, it's rare that any have coached more than two teams from the Original Six era. The most Original Six teams coached by one individual is three: The legendary **Dick Irvin Sr.** led Chicago, Toronto and Montreal during the 1930s, '40s and '50s; more recently, **Pat Burns** coached Montreal, Toronto and Boston in the 1980s, '90s and 2000.

**7.5**    Washington's **Brendan Witt** scored only eight points in 77 games but led the NHL in legal hits in 1999–2000. Witt, a Canadian major junior first team All-Star in 1994, delivered a league-high 322 blows to the opposition.

**7.6**    The nickname was applied to Bure after his electrifying NHL debut with the Vancouver Canucks, in a game against the Winnipeg Jets November 5, 1991. The 20-year-old Russian wowed both the Vancouver crowd and the Jets with a series of thrilling rushes, prompting *Vancouver Sun* **sportswriter Iain MacIntyre** to note the next day: "If Winnipeg are the Jets, then what do you call Pavel Bure? How about the Rocket? It fits Bure perfectly. He is the fastest Soviet creation since *Sputnik*." The name stuck and soon the hockey world was calling Bure the Russian Rocket. As Kerry Banks noted in *Pavel Bure: The Riddle of the Russian Rocket*: "With its rolling alliteration and dual allusions to Cold War weaponry and supersonic speed, the moniker had an irresistible appeal."

**7.7**    Small players (under six feet, 190 pounds) have always been a part of the NHL. But in 1999–2000 a new generation of mighty mites, led by five-foot-six, 180-pound **Theo Fleury**, made big contributions to the success of their teams. Players such as Calgary's Valeri Bure (five foot ten), Detroit's Igor Larionov (five foot nine), Los Angeles' Zigmund Palffy (five foot 10), Philadelphia's Mark Recchi (five foot 10), Pittsburgh's Martin Straka (five foot 10), Boston Sergei Samsonov (five foot eight) and

Montreal's Saku Koivu (five foot 10) started a resurgence of the smaller, skilled player. In fact, small players have decreased the NHL's average weight by 1.8 pounds to a low of 199.3 pounds, the biggest decrease in 26 years.

**7.8** The first hat trick in the Thrashers' history was scored by rookie **Dean Sylvester** November 22, 1999, in a 6–3 win over Vancouver. Sylvester's four points (he also registered an assist) were his first in the NHL. It was just his fourth NHL start.

**7.9** Although the Canadiens have had a few stiffs over the years, there is no denying the club has had a steady stream of successes between the pipes. Montreal's roster of backstoppers, from Georges Vezina to George Hainsworth, Bill Durnan, Jacques Plante, Ken Dryden and Patrick Roy, reads like a *Who's Who* of netminding All-Stars. Montreal's good fortune has come, in part, from **smart drafting, a little luck and a stable of talent in its own backyard.** For example, in 1999–2000 there were 10 goaltenders from Quebec playing in the NHL.

**7.10** One of the few NHL records still held by the great **Maurice Richard** is his six playoff overtime goals. Richard scored the six winners in only 133 postseason contests. Runner-up Glenn Anderson notched five in 225 games. Richard, hockey's purest goal scorer, potted one sudden-death goal in 1946, three in 1951, one in 1957 and his last in 1958.

**7.11** **Bobby Orr** won eight straight Norris Trophies between 1968 and 1975. Second in Norris wins is Montreal's Doug Harvey, who received the honour as top defenseman seven times during the 1950s and 1960s, followed by Ray Bourque with five.

**7.12** **Milan Hejduk** notched the first goal at the Colorado Avalanche's new home, the Pepsi Center, October 13, 1999, but he wasn't the last goal scorer at NcNichols Arena (as is sometimes reported). However, the Czech winger did earn an assist on the last regular-season goal, which was scored by Theo Fleury April 18, 1999. So, Hejduk can claim to be the only player to register a regular-season point on the last goal at McNichols Arena and the first goal at the Pepsi Center. (For the record, the final goal at McNichols Arena was scored six weeks later on June 1 in Game 6 of the Western Conference finals by Dallas' **Richard Matvichuk.**)

**7.13** New Jersey's **Scott Gomez** is believed to be the first Mexican-American to play in the NHL. Born in Alaska, Gomez turned in the hottest performance by a rookie in 1999–2000 with a league-leading 70 points on 19 goals and 51 assists. Commenting on his Latino status, Gomez said, "It's not like I'm breaking any barriers, not like Jackie Robinson."

**7.14** The Stanley Cup has a way of following some players around. Hard-nosed **Mike Keane**, the ultimate depth player, is one of those lucky few. Keane is the only player during the 1990s to win Stanley Cups on three different teams: Montreal in 1993, Colorado in 1996 and Dallas in 1999.

**7.15** A few players have since equalled or bettered Lafleur's 28-game scoring streak, but the first was **Wayne Gretzky,** who broke the Flower's NHL mark in 1982–83 with a 30-game drive that earned him 76 points. Lafleur scored 61 points during his 1976–77 streak.

**7.16** The Canadiens are no longer the Flying Frenchmen of their glorious dynasty years. In 1999–2000, only four regulars— **Patrice Brisebois, Benoit Brunet, Patrick Bouillon and Jose Theodore**—were French-speaking players. As further proof of the malaise affecting the once-great Canadiens: Before the Leafs traded defenseman Sylvain Cote to Chicago, the Quebec-City native nixed the idea of coming to Montreal by insisting on a trade to an American club. "To come here [Montreal] would have been a big distraction. It's hard for a French-Canadian player to play here," explained Cote.

**7.17**  Colorado's **Chris Drury** is the only player to win both the Hobey Baker (1998) and the Calder Trophy (1999). Drury, who won the coveted honours in back-to-back years, was a scoring leader at Boston University before joining Colorado in 1998–99. Drury scored 44 points in 79 games with the Avalanche to claim the top rookie honour.

**7.18**  Hank Aaron and Don Cherry were **born on the same date,** February 5, 1934. But although both are Aquarians, there is very little else these sports giants have in common, especially in their fields of play. Aaron hit a major-league record 755 home runs in his career; Cherry scored no goals in his one NHL start. Aaron comes from Mobile, Alabama; Cherry from Kingston, Ontario.

**7.19**  Seven NHL games were played on January 1, 2000, two of which were afternoon games: Tampa Bay in Florida and San Jose in Nashville. The Predators-Sharks tangled at 2 p.m. eastern standard time, one hour earlier than the Panthers-Lightning game that got underway at 3 p.m. at Florida's National Car Rental Center. Based on these starts, the first goal scored in Nashville would be the new millennium's first NHL goal. That distinction went to the Predators' **Sergei Krivokrasov,** who scored at 0:22 of the first period in the 3–2 win over San Jose.

**7.20**  Only a handful of goalies have scored an NHL goal, and Patrick Roy is not among that group. Not that the Avalanche goalie hasn't attempted to join. Near the end of one game on April 3, 1999, with Colorado leading 4–2 and Edmonton going with the extra man, Roy shot a number of times from outside his crease at the vacated Oiler net. He didn't succeed, but he did raise the ire of the Oilers. "He's got an ego bigger than the Goodyear blimp," cussed Edmonton assistant coach Ted Green.

# Game 7

# HOCKEY CROSSWORD 2

*(Solutions are on page 121)*

### Across

1. Felix "_____" Potvin

5. Chicago D-man Cam _____

9. Period of time, the six-team _____

10. Canuck city

11. Fast-paced style of play

12. Opposite of West

14. Last playoff round

16. Game official

19. Goalie ironman from 1950s, '60s (2 words)

20. Break up or _____ the defense

22. After an injury a player goes into _____

24. Area between bluelines (2 words)

26. What a player needs for a long season

27. Old-timer Babe _____

29. Seven-team journeyman from 1970s, Bobby _____

30. Illegal stick move; he was _____

### Down

1. George "_____" Armstrong

2. No leniency: Zero _____

3. Sign up again or _____ a contract

4. Montreal's Brian _____

5. 1990s fourth-line winger with Habs, Ed _____

6. A 0–0 game is _____

7. 1980s Minnesota-Calgary centre, Mike _____

8. Donator of Cup, _____ Stanley

13. Shots _____ goal

15. Philly's goalie, Pelle
   _____

17. New York team

18. Long-term or _____ -_____
   contract (2 words)

19. Old Maple Leaf
   _____

21. Part of foot

23. 1970s Boston's Ken
   _____

24. Another kick at the
   _____

25. 1970s Ranger goalie,
   _____ Giacomin

28. Colour of centre-ice line
   _____

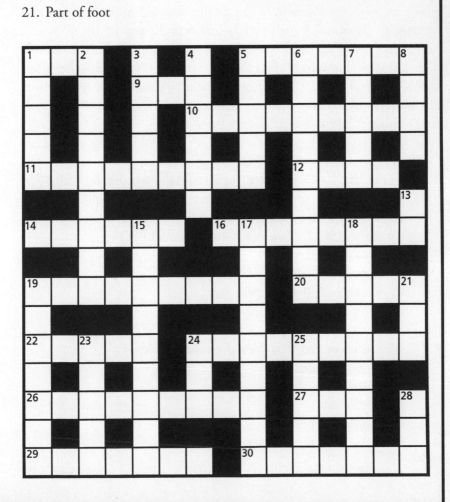

# 8
# SOFT ICE

For the second time in four years the Boston Bruins failed to make the playoffs in 1999–2000, but for Joe Thornton, the NHL's number-one overall draft pick of 1997, things looked pretty good. In the last game, a 3–1 victory over Pittsburgh, the Bruins forward notched a goal and an assist to give him 23 goals and 37 assists in the season, the 60 points he needed to collect a U.S.$1.4-million incentive bonus. Over the sound system boomed Pink Floyd's "Money." "I couldn't help but smile," Thornton said. "It's going to be a nice summer for me." Before our playoff questions in the next chapter, stickhandle past this miscellany of hockey trivia. Watch out for the soft ice.

(*Answers are on page ...* )

**8.1** In the Kansas City Blades' regular-season IHL finale April 17, 1999, the club sponsored a promotion called Toothless Night, where fans with missing teeth got in for free. How many among the 9,325 fans in attendance qualified?
A. Less than 40 fans
B. Between 40 and 400 fans
C. Between 400 and 1,000 fans
D. More than 1,000 fans

**8.2** Who was the only NHL penalty leader picked in the NHL draft's first round?
A. Marty McSorley
B. Tie Domi
C. Jimmy Mann
D. Bob Probert

**8.3** What is the Web site *www.nogoal.com* dedicated to?
   A. NHLers who have never scored a goal
   B. Goals disallowed by video replay
   C. The Stanley Cup-winning goal of 1999
   D. NHL shutout records

**8.4** How much does it cost the general public to rent ice time at the Toronto Maple Leafs' former home, Maple Leaf Gardens?
   A. $602.50 per hour
   B. $802.50 per hour
   C. $1,002.50 per hour
   D. $1,202.50 per hour

**8.5** In 1999–2000, hockey fanatic Taylor Railton visited every NHL arena to see each of the league's teams play a home game. How did he travel?
   A. By car
   B. By plane
   C. By train
   D. By bicycle

**8.6** How long was it before Gordie Howe's parents saw their son playing in an NHL game?
   A. One season
   B. Three seasons
   C. 13 seasons
   D. Howe's parents never saw him play in the NHL

**8.7** What is the value of the most expensive hockey trading card?
   A. $10,000
   B. $20,000
   C. $30,000
   D. $40,000

**8.8** Who is the highest overall pick among NHL penalty leaders?

A. Dave Williams

B. Jimmy Mann

C. Tie Domi

D. Steve Durbano

**8.9** What is the most number of NHL arenas played in by a player during his career?

A. Less than 25 arenas

B. Between 25 and 35 arenas

C. Between 35 and 45 arenas

D. More than 45 arenas

**8.10** In the NHL version of Monopoly, the board game, what two franchises occupy Boardwalk and Park Place?

A. The New York Rangers and the Montreal Canadiens

B. The Montreal Canadiens and the Toronto Maple Leafs

C. The Toronto Maple Leafs and the Detroit Red Wings

D. The Detroit Red Wings and the Los Angeles Kings

**8.11** One of hockey's most enduring images is of tough guy Tiger Williams riding his stick between his legs (like a witch on a broom) after scoring a big goal. How often does Williams claim he performed that celebration in his career?

A. He claims to have done it only once

B. He claims to have done it after every first goal of a new season

C. He claims to have done it after every regular-season goal

D. He claims to have done it after every playoff goal

**8.12** According to a 1998–99 survey of hockey arenas worldwide, which statement is correct?

A. Canada has 300 indoor rinks; Russia has 2,840
B. Canada has 1,300 indoor rinks; Russia has 1,840
C. Canada has 2,300 indoor rinks: Russia has 840
D. Canada has 3,300 indoor rinks; Russia has 84

**8.13** During its inaugural season, 1999–2000, in Raleigh, North Carolina, the Hurricanes averaged how many empty seats per night?

A. 4,000 empty seats
B. 6,000 empty seats
C. 8,000 empty seats
D. 10,000 empty seats

**8.14** In a 1999 search for the top Zamboni driver of the year, how many votes did winner Jimmy "The Iceman" MacNeil receive?

A. Less than 1,000 votes
B. Between 1,000 and 100,000 votes
C. Between 100,000 and 250,000 votes
D. More than 250,000 votes

**8.15** Who was the last member of the gold-medal-winning 1980 U.S. Olympic team to be active in the NHL?

A. Mike Ramsey
B. Neal Broten
C. Ken Morrow
D. Mark Pavelich

**8.16** What job did Teemu Selanne have in Finland before he joined the NHL in 1992?

A. Bartender
B. Fire fighter
C. Postal worker
D. Kindergarten teacher

**8.17** How much money was bid at a team charity auction in 2000 for dinner with Florida star Pavel Bure?
A. $2,500
B. $4,500
C. $6,500
D. $8,500

**8.18** After a number of high-profile stick-swinging incidents in 1999–2000, the NHL made it onto "The Late Show with David Letterman" in unceremonious fashion. In Letterman's list of top-10 new NHL slogans, what was his number one NHL slogan?
A. Dirtiest Game on Earth
B. Stick It to Me, Baby
C. We Will, We Will Sock You
D. He Shoots, He Scars

# SOFT ICE
## Answers

**8.1** **B. Between 40 and 400 fans**
They called it a promotion with real bite. A total of 269 fans were admitted free as part of Toothless Night at the Blades' final home game of 1998–99. Another 48 fans with a chipped tooth qualified for a half-price deal. No one bothered to count the number of dentists in attendance.

**8.2** **C. Jimmy Mann**
Mann, a hard-hitting winger and first team All-Star with the Sherbrooke Beavers in the Quebec juniors, was Winnipeg's first choice, 19th overall at the 1979 draft. Mann had size, toughness and potential, but after leading the league with 287 penalty minutes during his first year, he never managed a full

NHL season again. He was later traded to Quebec to become the team's designated fighter.

**8.3    C.  The Stanley Cup-winning goal of 1999**

After the Dallas Stars won the Stanley Cup on Brett Hull's so-called "tainted goal" (yes, Brett's foot was in the crease but he had control of the puck), Buffalo fan Jeffrey Spring designed a Web page "so that people won't forget the only time they didn't finish the Stanley Cup finals," said Spring. The site *www.nogoal.com* offered surfers the famous overhead shot of Hull's goal, plus "No Goal" T-shirts, caps, and bumper stickers.

**8.4    B.  $802.50 per hour**

Ever since the Maple Leafs skated off to the Air Canada Centre and abandoned their old home at Carlton and Church, Maple Leaf Gardens has been a dark and silent place. It still hosts the occasional Junior A and lacrosse match, but, for the most part, Canada's most famous hockey shrine is like a puck without a stick. The NHL's loss is the public's gain. For an $802.50-per-hour rental rate, non-NHLers can now skate and shoot in the glorious tracks of some of the game's greatest players, from Charlie Conacher to Mats Sundin. There are a few annoying rules, however. Among them: No pegs are provided for the nets, no spectators are allowed, and there is a maximum of 22 skaters per session.

**8.5    A.  By car**

It was the road trip of a lifetime. Taylor Railton, a 67-year-old Philadelphia native, completed his eight-week, 18,000-mile cross-country odyssey in a 1995 Ford Taurus. The $6,000 trip began in Philadelphia on January 1; before it was over on February 24, Railton had been profiled on television and in newspapers and had met many hockey legends, including Phil Esposito, Denis Potvin and Bryan Trottier. His Taurus went through three oil changes and plenty of Celine Dion tapes (to help him "relax" out on the road). The best hot dogs? Montreal. The worst? New Jersey ("The bun was cold.").

**8.6    C.   13 seasons**

According to Howe, Gordie's dad never saw him play more than 10 times. The first occasion was for "Gordie Howe Night" in Detroit, March 3, 1959. Before game time, Howe received a new car. To his surprise, sitting in the back seat were his parents, Catherine and Ab, who travelled from Saskatchewan for the ceremony. It was Howe's 13th season, more than twice the average span of an NHL career.

**8.7    B.   $20,000**

While Bobby Orr's rookie card is often cited as the most valuable hockey card available in stores, it is not the most highly priced card. Instead, a defenseman from the NHL's first decade—Bert Corbeau of the 1923–24 Toronto St. Pats—graces the cardboard of hockey's top card. Only 10 Corbeau cards are known to exist.

---

### THE TOP 10 MOST VALUABLE HOCKEY CARDS*

| | | | |
|---|---|---|---|
| 1. Bert Corbeau | V145-1 | 1923–24 | $20,000 |
| 2. Georges Vezina | C55 | 1911–12 | $5,000 |
| 3. Howie Morenz | V145-1 | 1923–24 | $3,000 |
| 4. Gordie Howe | Parkhurst | 1951–52 | $3,000 |
| 5. Bobby Hull | Topps | 1958–59 | $3,000 |
| 6. Bobby Orr | Topps | 1966–67 | $2,500 |
| 7. Eddie Shore | V-129 | 1933–34 | $2,000 |
| 8. King Clancy | V-145-1 | 1923–24 | $1,700 |
| 9. Maurice Richard | Parkhurst | 1951–52 | $1,600 |
| 10. Aurel Joliat | V-145-1 | 1923–24 | $1,300 |

Note: "C" sets were issued by cigarette companies; "V" sets by confectionary companies.

*Beckett Hockey Card Price Guide

**8.8  D.  Steve Durbano**

Jimmy Mann is the only first-round pick to become an NHL penalty leader, but the top overall pick from that category is Steve Durbano. Durbano, chosen 13th overall by the New York Rangers in 1971, led the league in penalties with 370 in 1975–76, a season split between Pittsburgh (161) and the Kansas City Scouts (209). Mann was selected 19th overall in 1974, Dave Williams, 31st in 1974, and Tie Domi, 27th in 1988.

**8.9  D.  More than 45 arenas**

There are no official league records of such trivia, but in this ice age of new franchises and buildings, a few veterans have broken the plus-50 mark in rinks played in. In 1999–2000 at least four players, three of them Sharks, hit the 50-rink milestone. San Jose's Gary Suter and Ron Sutter bagged number 50 at Phillips Arena in Atlanta February 11, 2000; Vincent Damphousse followed with his 50th NHL arena shortly after. On February 13, 2000, Larry Murphy stepped onto the ice at Denver's Pepsi Center to play hockey on his 50th NHL rink. Murphy has also skated in a few neutral-site games in extinct venues in Atlanta and Cleveland. What are the 20-year veteran's favourite and least-favourite haunts? Old Maple Leaf Gardens in Toronto is a fond memory, and not because of the booing he received as a Maple Leaf but because it was where he saw his first game as a child. Calgary's Stampede Corral was a bust. The rink was small, the boards a foot higher than normal and the player benches were two parallel rows, which forced players in the back row to climb by players in the front to get to the ice.

**8.10  B.  The Montreal Canadiens and the Toronto Maple Leafs**

In 1999, Parker Brothers, the makers of Monopoly, issued an NHL hockey version of the popular board game. It was the first Monopoly game devoted to a professional league. Players in the game become team owners who can buy and sell franchises, acquire broadcasting partners and hammer out deals in arena luxury boxes. The two most prestigious properties, Boardwalk and Park Place, are occupied by hockey's two oldest franchises, the Canadiens and the Maple Leafs.

**8.11  A.  He claims to have done it only once**
Sports has witnessed many memorable post-score celebrations. In the initial euphoria, fists are pumped, balls spiked, crowds saluted, sticks raised and struts performed. It's the dance of high-five glory. Showboating. Well-remembered by hockey fans is Tiger Williams' wild stick ride after he scored the winning goal at 1998's old-timers All-Star game. Williams, the game's most incarcerated player (almost 4,000 career penalty minutes) and longtime Toronto fan favourite, was making his first appearance back at Maple Leaf Gardens after his trade to Vancouver. In his moment of ecstasy, Williams spontaneously turned, tucked his stick between his legs, squatted and rode the shaft around the rink—to the jubilation of thousands. His act of on-ice ingenuity was seared into the brains of kids across the country, who watched it on TV replays. "Everybody … thinks that this happened hundreds and hundreds of times," Williams told the *National Post*. "But I only did it once. That's the greatest thing about it. When you do something and it's unique, it sticks in the memory for a long time."

**8.12  D.  Canada has 3,300 indoor rinks; Russia has 84**
Canadians may not dominate the NHL like they once did nor lead the world in international play, but when it comes to arenas, Canada ranks number one by a huge edge. The survey, conducted by the International Ice Hockey Federation, listed Canada with 3,300 indoor-ice facilities; the United States with 1,500; and Russia, just 84.

**8.13  B.  6,000 empty seats**
Although the Hurricanes' move into Raleigh's Entertainment and Sports Arena increased attendance by 4,280 fans (a 54 per cent

jump, from 7,909 to 12,189, over the previous year), the club sold out only a few games all season, including the October 29 inaugural match. Carolina averaged 6,000 empty seats per night in its new 18,730-seat arena.

**8.14  C.  Between 100,000 and 250,000 votes**
When California-based Zamboni announced its search for the top driver of 2000, with the winner to clean the ice at the NHL All-Star game in Toronto, a number of candidates, including celebrities such as Garth Brooks and Bill Murray, received nominations. In time, the contest turned into a two-man race between Jimmy "The Iceman" MacNeil of the Brantford Civic Centre in Ontario, and legendary Detroit Red Wings iceman Al Sobotka. The Zamboni Web site received more than a million hits during the campaign; MacNeil's 177,566 votes eclipsed Sobotka's by an easy 80,000.

**8.15  B.  Neal Broten**
A few members of 1980's "Miracle on Ice" Olympic champions had real NHL potential, including Ken Morrow (1979 to 1989), Mark Pavelich (1981 to 1992), Craig Ramsey (1979 to 1997) and Neal Broten (1980 to 1997). Both Ramsey and Broten played in 1996–97, but Ramsey skated in just two games for Detroit that season before hanging up his jersey. Broten's 1996–97 season lasted longer: 42 games split between New Jersey, Los Angeles and Dallas.

**8.16  D.  Kindergarten teacher**
While playing for Helsinki Jokerit in the Finnish elite league, Teemu Selanne also taught kindergarten for three years. The kids knew about his night job, but didn't fully understand what was involved. Said Selanne, "When I left for the game they would say, 'Hey Teemu, score a thousand goals.'" Today, Selanne still keeps in touch with his former students, who follow his career in the newspapers and on the Internet.

**8.17  C. $6,500**

At a Panthers charity auction in February 2000, the bidding reached $6,500 for dinner with the Russian Rocket. Then, Bure's girlfriend, tennis star Anna Kournikova, hopped onto the stage alongside the Florida sniper and the price nearly doubled to $12,500. The highest bidder won a dinner for eight, including the two celebrity athletes, at Bure's favourite restaurant in South Beach, Florida.

**8.18  D.  He Shoots, He Scars**

If we could fast forward through 1999–2000, we'd see a train wreck of concussions, suspensions and player violence almost unparalleled in NHL history. We'd zap from Mike Modano's near career-ending crash into the boards courtesy of Ruslan Salei's hit from behind, to Marty McSorley's two-hander across the temple of Donald Brashear, to Ed Belfour's assault on hotel security

---

### LETTERMAN'S TOP 10 NHL SLOGANS

10. It's Like an Episode of 'Cops' on Ice
 9. See for Yourself What Canadian Blood Looks Like
 8. The 'H' Is for 'Hematoma'
 7. It's Like Watching Really, Really Primitive Dentistry
 6. A Sport That Combines Your Two Favourite Things: Ice Skating and Head Trauma
 5. You Can't Spell 'Unhealthy' Without 'NHL'
 4. Share the Excitement or We'll Beat Your Brains in with a Piece of Wood
 3. We Injure More People by 9 p.m. Than Pro Football Does All Year
 2. Don't Worry, Kids—They're Just Saying 'Puck'
 1. He Shoots, He Scars

---

guards and his mace-in-the-face arrest to Bryan Berard's sickening stick-in-the-eye injury, to Scott Neidermayer's clubbing of Peter Worrell and Worrell's subsequent throat-slashing gesture directed at the Devils' bench, and finally to numerous hospital head-trauma units where Eric Lindros, Jaromir Jagr and Peter Forsberg all spent time with concussions. It would be a gruesome view of hockey. As a poignant close, the finale would go to David Letterman's top 10 list.

# SOLUTIONS TO GAMES

## Game 1: Hockey Crossword 1

| L | O | S | A | N | G | E | L | E | S | K | I | N | G | S |
|---|---|---|---|---|---|---|---|---|---|---|---|---|---|---|
| I | T |   |   | A |   | N |   |   | N | A | M | E |   | E |
| N | E | E | L | Y |   | R | O | D |   | T |   | S |   | T |
| D | V |   | O | H | L |   | T | H | R | I | L | L | S |   |
| B | E |   | U |   | Y |   | O |   | A |   | U |   |   |   |
| E | R |   | N |   |   | H | E | A | D | I | N | G |   |   |
| R | S |   | G | R | E | E | N |   | E |   | D | I | T |   |
| G | O | O | N |   | E |   | D | D |   | L |   |   |   |   |
| H |   | N | I | L | A | N |   | P | R | E | S | L | E | Y |
|   | L |   | N |   | R |   | A | L |   | A |   | U | S | A |
| L | O | S | E |   | D | E | M | A | N | D |   | D |   | W |
|   | O | T |   | R | O | D |   | Y |   | L |   | W |   | N |
|   | B | E | H | I | N | D |   |   | I |   | I | C | E |   |
|   | V |   | C |   | I | R | V | I | N |   | G | U | Y |   |
| B | R | E | A | K |   | E |   |   | E | D |   | T |   |   |

## Game 2: Strange Starts

### Part 1

1. D. Brett Hull, Calgary Flames
2. G. Cam Neely, Vancouver Canucks
3. F. Reggie Leach, Boston Bruins
4. C. Adam Oates, Detroit Red Wings
5. B. Tony Esposito, Montreal Canadiens
6. A. Rick Middleton, New York Rangers
7. E. Randy Carlyle, Toronto Maple Leafs

### Part 2

1. B. Dominik Hasek, Chicago Blackhawks
2. G. Eddie Shack, New York Rangers
3. E. Rick Kehoe, Toronto Maple Leafs
4. F. Bernie Parent, Boston Bruins
5. A. Mats Sundin, Quebec Nordiques
6. D. Teemu Selanne, Winnipeg Jets
7. C. Marcel Dionne, Detroit Red Wings

## Game 3: American Olympians

BROTE**N**
CHE**L**I**O**S
**P**AVELI**C**H
GR**AN**ATO
**T**K**A**CHUK
LE**E**T**C**H
IA**FRA**TE

**PAT LAFONTAINE**

## Game 4: Captains of Time

1. K. Johnny Bucyk, 11 years with Boston
2. D. George Armstrong, 12 years with Toronto
3. J. Pierre Pilote, seven seasons with Chicago
4. I. Alex Delvecchio, 11 years with Detroit
5. B. Jean Béliveau, 10 years with Montreal
6. H. Bob Gainey, eight seasons with Montreal
7. E. Bill Cook, 11 years with New York
8. F. Brian Sutter, nine years with St. Louis
9. G. Hap Day, 10 years with Toronto
10. C. Stan Smyl, nine years with Vancouver
11. A. Rod Langway, 11 seasons with Washington

# Game 5: The Puck Puzzle

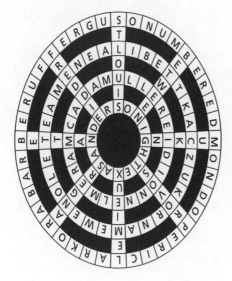

# Game 6: Unusual Endings

**Part 1**

1. D. Gordie Howe, Hartford Whalers
2. A. Larry Robinson, Los Angeles Kings
3. F. Jacques Plante, Boston Bruins
4. G. Darryl Sittler, Detroit Red Wings
5. H. Pierre Pilote, Toronto Maple Leafs
6. C. Steve Smith, Calgary Flames
7. E. Doug Harvey, St. Louis Blues
8. B. Bobby Orr, Chicago Blackhawks

**Part 2**

1. E. Guy Lafleur, Quebec Nordiques
2. F. Borje Salming, Detroit Red Wings
3. A. Bobby Hull, Hartford Whalers
4. B. Dale Hunter, Colorado Avalanche
5. C. Andy Bathgate, Pittsburgh Penguins
6. D. Peter Stastny, St. Louis Blues
7. H. Rick Martin, Los Angeles Kings
8. G. Denis Savard, Tampa Bay Lightning

# Game 7: Hockey Crossword 2

# ACKNOWLEDGEMENTS

The author gratefully acknowledges the help of Steve Dryden and everyone at the *Hockey News*; Gary Meagher and Benny Ercolani of the NHL; Phil Prichard and Craig Campbell at the Hockey Hall of Fame; the staff at the McLellan-Redpath Library at McGill University; Floyd Whitney in Edmonton; Rob Sanders and Terri Wershler at Greystone Books; the many hockey writers, broadcast-journalists, media and Internet organizations who have made the game better through their own work; as well as editors Anne Rose and Kerry Banks for their dedication, expertise and humour, fact-checker and nitpicker Kerry Banks, and graphic artist Peter van Vlaardingen and puzzle designer Adrian van Vlaardingen for their creativity.

Thanks to the following publishers and organizations for the use of quoted and statistical material:

- *Beckett Hockey Card Price Guide.*
- *The Death of Hockey.* By Jeff Z. Klein and Karl-Eric Reif. Published by Macmillan Canada (1998).
- *The Hockey News,* various excerpts. Reprinted by permission of the *Hockey News,* a division of GTC Transcontinental Publishing, Inc.
- *The Montreal Gazette.* Published by Southam, Inc.
- *The National Post.*
- *Pavel Bure: The Riddle of the Russian Rocket.* By Kerry Banks. Published by Greystone Books (1999).
- *The St. Louis Post-Dispatch.*
- *Total Hockey.* By Dan Diamond and Associates, Inc. Published by Total Sports (1998).
- *Where Are They Now? A Celebration of the Best on Ice.* By John Crosato, Raye Hollitt, and Bert Ridd. Published by Where Are They Now? Inc.

Care has been taken to trace ownership of copyright material contained in this book. The publishers welcome any information that will enable them to rectify any reference or credit in subsequent editions.